AGRICULTURE ISSUES AND POLICIES

FEDERAL CROP INSURANCE

BACKGROUND AND COSTS OF INSURING HIGHER PRODUCTION RISKS

AGRICULTURE ISSUES AND POLICIES

Additional books in this series can be found on Nova's website under the Series tab.

Additional e-books in this series can be found on Nova's website under the e-book tab.

AGRICULTURE ISSUES AND POLICIES

FEDERAL CROP INSURANCE

BACKGROUND AND COSTS OF INSURING HIGHER PRODUCTION RISKS

AUDREY POPE
EDITOR

NOVINKA
New York

Library of Congress Cataloging-in-Publication Data

ISBN: 978-1-63483-366-0

Published by Nova Science Publishers, Inc. † New York

Contents

Preface **vii**

Chapter 1 Federal Crop Insurance: Background **1**
Dennis A. Shields

Chapter 2 Crop Insurance: In Areas with Higher Crop Production Risks, Costs Are Greater, and Premiums May Not Cover Expected Losses **33**
United States Government Accountability Office

Index **75**

PREFACE

The federal crop insurance program began in 1938 when Congress authorized the Federal Crop Insurance Corporation. The current program, which is administered by the U.S. Department of Agriculture's Risk Management Agency (RMA), provides producers with risk management tools to address crop yield and/or revenue losses for about 130 crops. The federal farm safety net also includes the farm commodity support programs, which provide price and income support for a much narrower list of "covered and loan commodities" such as corn, wheat, rice, and peanuts. This book provides a primer on the federal crop insurance program and highlights changes to the program by the 2014 farm bill. It also the examines the government's cost of the crop insurance program; and the extent to which RMA's premium rates, as implemented, cover expected losses.

In: Federal Crop Insurance
Editor: Audrey Pope
ISBN: 978-1-63483-366-0

Chapter 1

FEDERAL CROP INSURANCE: BACKGROUND*

Dennis A. Shields

SUMMARY

The federal crop insurance program began in 1938 when Congress authorized the Federal Crop Insurance Corporation. The current program, which is administered by the U.S. Department of Agriculture's Risk Management Agency (RMA), provides producers with risk management tools to address crop yield and/or revenue losses for about 130 crops. The federal farm safety net also includes the farm commodity support programs, which provide price and income support for a much narrower list of "covered and loan commodities" such as corn, wheat, rice, and peanuts.

In purchasing a crop insurance policy, a producer growing an insurable crop selects a level of coverage and pays a portion of the premium—or none of it in the case of catastrophic coverage— which increases as the level of coverage rises. The federal government pays the rest of the premium (62%, on average, in 2014). Insurance policies are sold and completely serviced through 18 approved private insurance companies. As spelled out in a Standard Reinsurance Agreement (SRA), the insurance companies' losses are reinsured by USDA, and their

* This is an edited, reformatted and augmented version of a Congressional Research Service publication R40532, prepared for Members and Committees of Congress, dated January 9, 2015.

administrative and operating costs are reimbursed by the federal government.

In 2014, federal crop insurance policies covered 294 million acres. Major crops are covered in most counties where they are grown. Four crops—corn, cotton, soybeans, and wheat—typically account for more than 70% of total acres enrolled in crop insurance. Most crop insurance policies are either yield-based or revenue-based. For yield-based policies, a producer can receive an indemnity if there is a yield (production) loss relative to the farmer's "normal" (historical) yield. Revenue-based policies protect against crop revenue loss resulting from declines in yield, price, or both. Other insurance products protect against losses in whole farm revenue (rather than just for an individual crop) or gross margins for livestock enterprises.

Government costs for crop insurance have increased substantially during the last decade. After ranging between $2.1 billion and $3.9 billion during FY2000-FY2007, costs rose to $7 billion in FY2009 as higher policy premiums from rising crop prices drove up premium subsidies to farmers and expense reimbursements (which are based on total premiums) to private insurance companies. Costs peaked at $14.1 billion in FY2012 when crop prices surged again and poor weather resulted in program losses. With a return to more favorable weather and smaller crop losses, total program costs declined to $6.0 billion in FY2013 and were $8.7 billion in FY2014.

Federal outlays for crop insurance exceed those for the farm commodity support programs, making crop insurance the most significant cost component of the farm safety net and a potential target for deficit reduction. Insurance companies, farm groups, and some Members of Congress are concerned that any reductions in federal support could negatively impact the financial health of the industry and possibly jeopardize the delivery of crop insurance to farmers. Supporters of federal crop insurance do not want to make changes that would adversely affect farmer participation, policy coverage, or industry interest in selling and servicing insurance products to farmers. Critics argue that premium subsidies are higher than necessary for farmers to adequately protect themselves, and significant federal dollars could be saved if subsidies were lowered. From a farm policy standpoint, policy makers and observers alike remain concerned about how the crop insurance program interacts with farm commodity support programs and whether together they help farmers deal with business risk at a cost that is acceptable to taxpayers.

In the 2014 farm bill (P.L. 113-79), Congress expanded the federal crop insurance program by authorizing additional policies and requiring examination of potential new products, including those that would benefit specialty crops and animal agriculture.

For many farmers, federal crop insurance is the most important component of the farm safety net, given the breadth of commodity coverage, from apples to wheat, and the capability to reimburse producers for crop losses. The federal crop insurance program makes available subsidized policies to help farmers manage risk associated with natural disasters, including drought, excess moisture, and other perils. The average annual federal cost is approximately $8 billion.

This report provides a primer on the federal crop insurance program and highlights changes to the program by the 2014 farm bill (P.L. 113-79).

The farm safety net also includes the farm commodity support programs, which provide price and income support for a much narrower list of "covered and loan commodities" such as corn, soybeans, wheat, rice, and peanuts. Agricultural disaster programs are available for producers owning livestock or fruit trees.

CROP INSURANCE HISTORY

Farming is generally regarded as a financially risky enterprise. Most agricultural production is subject to the vagaries of weather, and shifts in agricultural supply and demand often result in volatile market prices. Farm financial risk, periods of low returns, and the importance of agriculture in the nation's economy during the early to mid-1900s led to the development of federal policies that financially supported farmers, primarily through commodity price mechanisms. Today's farm commodity policies—authorized in the 2014 farm bill—have their roots in the 1930s.

During the same era, Congress also first authorized federal crop insurance as an experiment to address the effects of the Great Depression and crop losses seen in the Dust Bowl. In 1938, the Federal Crop Insurance Corporation (FCIC) was created to carry out the program, which focused on major crops in major producing regions. The availability of federal crop insurance remained limited until passage of the Federal Crop Insurance Act of 1980 (P.L. 96-365), which expanded crop insurance to many more crops and regions of the country. Congress enhanced the crop insurance program, including greater subsidy levels, in 1994 and again in 2000 in order to encourage greater participation. The changes also expanded the role of the private sector in developing new products that would help farmers manage their risks.[1] Today, many banks, when making operating loans, require that farmers purchase crop insurance.

The federal crop insurance program is permanently authorized by the Federal Crop Insurance Act, as amended (7 U.S.C. 1501 et seq.). It is periodically modified. For example, Congress chose to revise the statute in the 2008 farm bill (P.L. 110-246) to achieve budget savings and to supplement crop insurance with a permanent disaster payment program. The 2014 farm bill (P.L. 113-79) expanded the program and increased budget outlays.[2] The U.S. Department of Agriculture's (USDA's) Risk Management Agency (RMA) operates and manages the FCIC.

PROGRAM BASICS

The federal crop insurance program provides producers with risk management tools to address crop yield and/or revenue losses on farms. Guarantees are established just prior to planting, based on historical yields and expected market prices (not statutory prices used in farm programs). Insurance policies are sold and completely serviced through 18 approved private insurance companies. Independent insurance agents are paid sales commissions by the companies. The insurance companies' losses are reinsured by USDA, and their administrative and operating costs are reimbursed by the federal government (see *Figure 1* and "Federal Program Costs," below).

In purchasing a policy, a producer growing an insurable crop selects a level of coverage and pays a portion of the premium, which increases as the level of coverage rises. The remainder of the premium is covered by the federal government (about 62% of total premium, on average, is paid by the government).[3] In the case of catastrophic coverage, the government pays the full premium. Also, the government, not the farmer, pays for the cost of selling and servicing all policies. In the absence of premium subsidies and free delivery, farmer participation in the crop insurance program and/or purchased coverage levels would be lower. A major benefit for producers is the timely payment for crop losses (about 30 days after the farmer signs the claim form).

In 2014, crop insurance policies covered 294 million acres (*Figure 2*). Major crops are insurable in most counties where they are grown, and approximately 83% of U.S. crop acreage is insured under the federal crop insurance program.[4] Four crops—corn, cotton, soybeans, and wheat—typically account for more than 70% of total enrolled acres. For these major crops, a large share of plantings is covered by crop insurance. In 2014, the portion of total corn acreage covered by federal crop insurance was 87%; cotton, 96%; soybeans, 88%; and wheat, 84%.

Policies for less widely produced crops are available in primary growing areas. Examples include dry peas, blueberries, citrus, pumpkins, and walnuts. In total, policies are available for about 130 crops (including coverage on a variety of fruit trees, nursery crops, pasture, rangeland, and forage).[5]

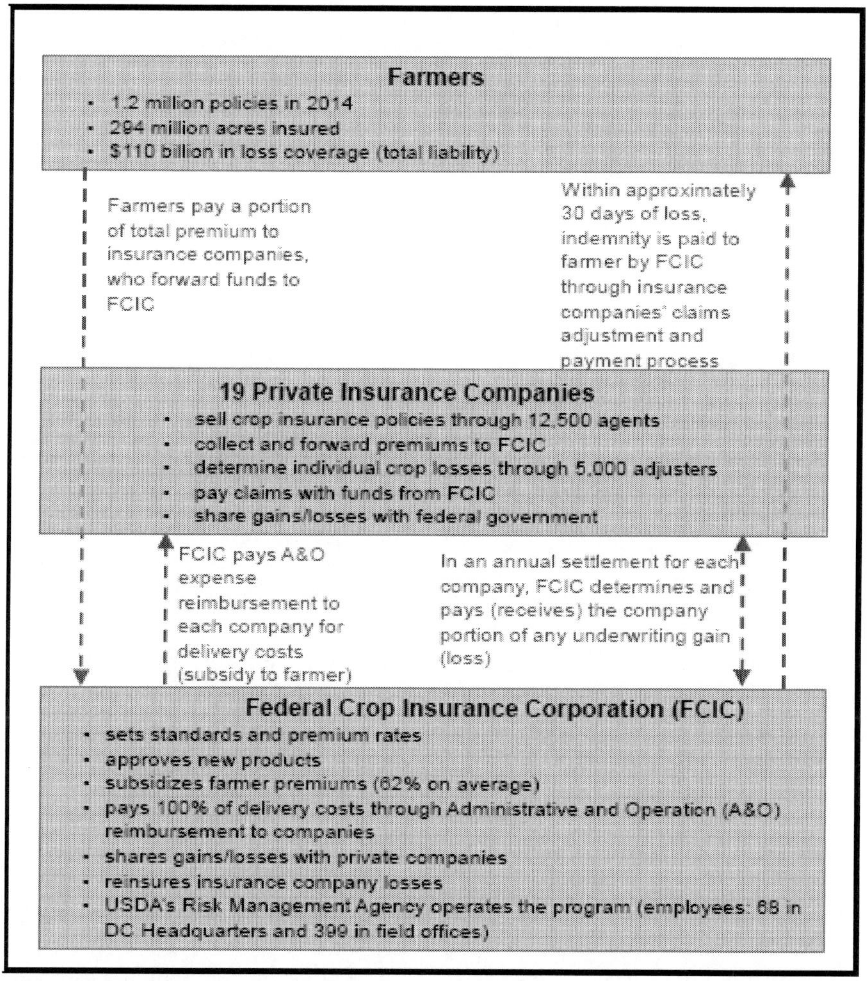

Source: CRS, adapted from U.S. Department of Agriculture and industry sources.

Figure 1. Federal Crop Insurance Program.

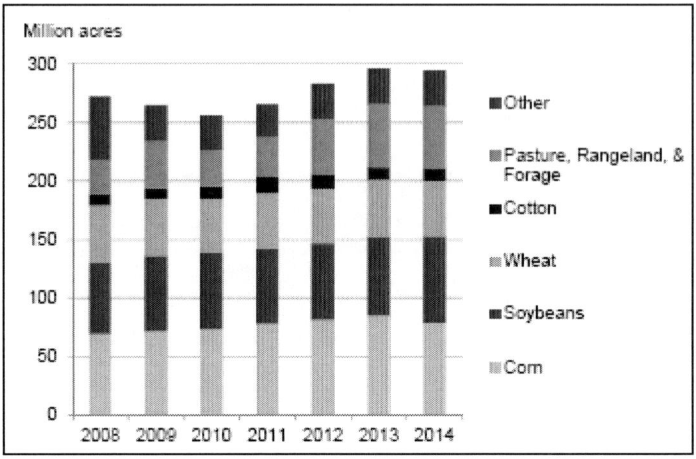

Source: U.S. Department of Agriculture, Risk Management Agency.

Figure 2. Insured Acres by Crop Year.

Many specialty crop producers depend on crop insurance as the only "safety net" for their operation, unlike field crop producers, who are also eligible for farm commodity program payments.[6] In the specialty crop category, insured acreage as a share of total acreage is 73% for fruits and nuts and 32% for vegetables.[7]

Crop insurance is not necessarily limited to crops. Relatively new or pilot programs protect livestock and dairy producers from loss of gross margin or price declines.[8] Livestock producers can also insure against hay and forage losses through the Pasture, Rangeland, and Forage program, which uses a rainfall index or vegetative index to determine loss.[9] A pilot program began in 2014 for annual hay production in North Dakota, South Dakota, Nebraska, Kansas, Oklahoma, and Texas.[10]

Policy Availability

The availability of crop insurance for a particular crop in a particular region is an administrative decision made by USDA. The decision is made on a crop-by-crop and county-by-county basis, based on farmer demand for coverage and the level of risk associated with the crop in the region, among other factors. Developing new products can be costly, and a significant challenge is obtaining credible data (yield and price) to create an actuarially sound product. The process usually starts with a pilot program, which is conducted for about three years in order for RMA to gain experience and test the program components before it becomes more widely available. Alternatively, a policy can be reviewed and later discontinued if it fails to perform at an acceptable level (e.g., low participation or high losses).

Some policies remain as a pilot for years. For example, the forage (alfalfa) seed insurance policy was introduced in 2002 as a pilot program to provide insurance coverage to alfalfa seed farmers. On May 29, 2014, USDA announced that it would be converted to a permanent policy for the 2015 crop year. During the pilot period, USDA determined an insurance need for hybrid production and made a program change to provide coverage for growers contracting for production of hybrid alfalfa seed.

Regions without Coverage

In regions where a policy is not available, farmers may request from the appropriate regional office that RMA expand the program to their county.[11] A producer also may request insurance coverage under a written agreement, which is a document designed to provide crop insurance for insurable crops when coverage or rates are unavailable.[12]

When crop insurance is not available, USDA's noninsured crop disaster assistance program (NAP) provides the equivalent of catastrophic coverage (for yield losses greater than 50%) if purchased by the producer. Additional coverage (for yield losses greater than 35%) has been made available by the 2014 farm bill. To be eligible for a NAP payment, a producer first must apply for coverage under the program by the application closing date, which varies by crop, but is generally about 30 days prior to the final planting date for an annual crop. As with catastrophic crop insurance, NAP applicants pay an administrative fee (currently $250 per crop). No premiums are required.[13]

Enhancing Existing Coverage

RMA also regularly responds to requests from commodity organizations or industry representatives for enhancements to existing coverage, such as adding revenue coverage and organic practice coverage or trend yield adjustments to better reflect a producer's liability. In some cases, RMA has not pursued policies for particular commodities because producers have expressed concerns that offering insurance could adversely affect the market (i.e., because an insurance policy reduces producer risk, farmers may plant more acreage, which could drive down prices and total crop revenue). This has been a concern for many vegetable crops and explains in part lower levels of insured vegetable acreage compared with other crops.[14]

Actuarial Soundness

Current law requires that RMA strive for actuarial soundness for the entire federal crop insurance program (that is, indemnities should equal total premiums, including premium subsidies).[15] As a result, RMA must set premium rates to only cover expected losses and a reasonable reserve. The agency is also required to conduct periodic reviews of its rate-setting methodology, which sets premium rates according to the average historical rate of loss (e.g., if policies pay out 10% of their value, on average, then the rate should be 10%). Based on a review completed in July 2011, RMA adjusted its methodology for several major commodities to give more weight to recent years and to make other changes.[16]

Types of Insurance

Federal crop insurance policies are generally either yield-based or revenue-based. For most yield-based policies, a producer can receive an indemnity if there is a yield loss relative to the farmer's "normal" (historical) yield. Revenue-based policies were developed after yield-based policies, in the mid-1990s, to protect against crop revenue loss resulting from declines during the growing season in yield, price, or both. The most recent addition has been products that protect against losses in whole farm revenue rather than just for an individual crop. For both yield- and revenue-based policies, the price used to set the guarantee is based only on the expected price for the upcoming season, and is reset every year. This is in contrast to farm programs which either have price guarantees set in statute or use historical average prices and are designed to protect against longer-term price declines.

These two basic forms—yield-based and revenue-based—are discussed below, followed by a brief explanation of whole farm insurance. The text boxes in this report entitled "Crop Insurance Examples: Yield-Based vs. Revenue-Based" and "Federal Crop Insurance: Range of Coverage and Policies" explain program operation within the two broad categories.

Slightly more than 1.2 million crop insurance policies were active in 2013, with revenue-based policies accounting for three-quarters of the total (*Figure*

3), and the remainder being yield-based policies. On a premium basis, revenue policies account for 84% of all policies.

Yield-Based Insurance

When purchasing a crop insurance policy, a producer is assigned (1) a "normal" crop yield based on the producer's actual production history, and (2) a price for his commodity based on estimated market conditions. The producer can then select a percentage of his normal yield to be insured and a percentage of the price he wishes to receive when crop losses exceed the selected loss threshold. The level of crop yield coverage is viewed by farmers as a critical feature of crop insurance, and a major determinant of whether a farmer will purchase insurance.[17]

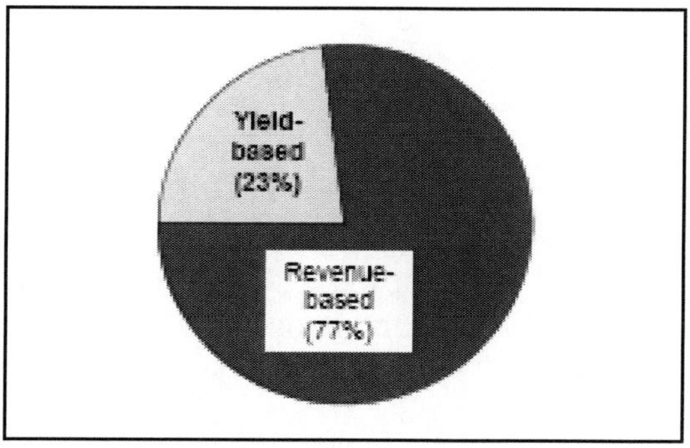

Source: U.S. Department of Agriculture, Risk Management Agency.

Notes: When calculated by share of premiums paid, yield-based policies account for 20% of total policies and revenue-based policies account for 80%. Index and "dollar" policies are included in yield-based total.

Figure 3. Types of Crop Insurance Policies. (policies earning premiums in 2014 = 1.2 million)

In determining what a normal production level is for an insurable farmer, USDA requires the producer to present actual annual crop yields (usually stated on a bushel-per-acre basis) for the last 4 to 10 years. The simple average of a producer's annual crop yield over this time period then serves as the producer's actual production history (APH). If a farmer does not have adequate records, he can be assigned a transition yield (T-yield) for each missing year of data, which is based on average county yields for the crop.

The most basic policy is called catastrophic (CAT) coverage. The premium for this level of coverage is completely subsidized by the federal government. The farmer pays an administrative fee for CAT coverage ($300 per crop per county), and in return can receive a payment on losses in excess of 50% of normal yield, equal to 55% of the estimated market price of the crop (called 50/55 coverage).

Coverage levels that are higher than CAT are called "buy-up" coverage, and most farmer purchase buy-up policies because of the additional protection.[18] For an additional premium paid by the producer, and partially subsidized by the government (see "Crop Insurance Premium Subsidies," below), a producer can "buy up" the 50/55 catastrophic coverage to any equivalent level of coverage between 50/100 and 75/100 (i.e., up to 75% of "normal" crop yield and 100% of the estimated market price). In limited areas, production can be insured up to the 85/100 level of coverage.

The policy name depends on how pricing is determined for the crop. "APH" policies use a projected price determined by RMA, while "Yield Protection" policies use a projected price based on the commodity exchange markets. For example, polices are APH for plums and Yield Protection for wheat.

Several other policies, including Area Yield Protection (formerly called Group Risk Plan) and Dollar Plan (see box), are not widely used but can be important for certain crops. Some of these policies use an area-wide index—such as county-level yield in the case of the Area Yield Protection—to measure losses.

Crop Insurance Examples:
Yield-Based vs. Revenue-Based

Two basic forms of crop insurance are yield-based and revenue-based. Yield-based insurance provides an indemnity when the actual yield falls below the guarantee level. Revenue-based insurance provides an indemnity when the revenue (actual yield x price) falls below the guarantee.

Actual Production History (APH) Example:

A loss occurs when the bushels of soybeans produced for the insurance unit (insurable acreage) fall below the production guarantee as a result of damage from a covered cause of loss. Assumptions: "normal" production = 48 bushels / acre; yield coverage level = 75%; established price coverage = 100%; price election = $9.90 / bushel; actual production = 20 bushels per acre.

48	bushels per acre APH yield
x .75	coverage level
36.0	bushel / acre guarantee
- 20.0	bushels / acre actually produced
16.0	bushels / acre of covered loss
x $9.90	per-bushel price election
$158.40	per-acre gross indemnity payment
- $6.00	estimated producer-paid premium per acre (varies)
$152.40	**per-acre net indemnity**

Revenue Product Example:

36.0	bushels / acre guarantee (see prior example)
x $11.00	per-bushel base price (announced in March)
$396.00	per-acre guarantee
20	bushels / acre actually produced
x $10.00	per-bushel harvest price (announced in November)
$200.00	per-acre revenue
$196.00	per-acre gross indemnity payment ($396.00 - $200.00)
- $13.00	estimated producer-paid premium (varies)
$183.00	**per-acre net indemnity**

Source: U.S. Department of Agriculture, Risk Management Agency, 2009 Commodity Insurance Fact Sheet - Soybeans - Iowa, January 2009, http://www.rma.usda.gov/fields/mn_rso/2009/2009iasoybeans.pdf.

Federal Crop Insurance: Range of Coverage and Policies

I. Catastrophic Coverage (CAT) pays 55% of the established price of the commodity on crop losses in excess of 50%, which is the deductible or out-of-pocket loss absorbed by farmer. The premium on CAT is paid by the federal government; however, producers must pay a $300 administrative fee for each crop insured in each county. Limited-resource and beginning farmers may have this fee waived. CAT coverage is not available on all types of policies.

II. Buy-up Coverage offers higher coverage (a lower deductible) and is purchased instead of CAT. Policies include: *Yield-based policies:*

Actual Production History (APH) and Yield Protection (YP) policies insure producers against yield losses due to natural causes such as drought, excessive moisture, hail, wind, frost, insects, and disease. The farmer selects the amount of average yield he or she wishes to insure, from 50% to 85%. The farmer also selects the percentage of the projected price he or she wants to insure—between 55% and 100% of the crop price (for APH, the price is established annually by RMA; for Yield Protection, the price is based on futures market prices). If the harvest is less than the yield insured, the farmer is paid an indemnity based on the difference. Indemnities are calculated by multiplying this difference by the insured percentage of the selected price.

Area Yield Protection (formerly Group Risk Plan or GRP) insures against widespread loss of production based on county average yields. When the county yield for the insured crop falls below the trigger level selected by the farmer, an indemnity is paid regardless of the individual farmer's actual yield. Coverage is available for up to 90% of the expected county yield. This protection involves less paperwork and costs less than the farm-level coverage described above. However, individual crop losses may not be covered if the county yield does not suffer a similar loss. This insurance is suitable for farmers whose crop losses typically follow the county pattern.

Dollar Plan provides protection against declining value due to damage that causes a yield shortfall. (Crop examples include cherries, chili peppers, citrus, and nursery crops.) Amount of insurance is based on the cost of growing a crop in a specific area. A loss occurs when the annual crop value is less than the amount of insurance. The maximum dollar amount of insurance is stated on the actuarial document. The insured may select a percentage of the maximum dollar amount equal to CAT (catastrophic level of coverage), or additional coverage levels.

The *Vegetation Index and Rainfall Index* do not measure direct production or loss; rather the farmer is insuring against an index that is expected to estimate production. The Pasture, Rangeland, and Forage (PRF) pilot program and the Apiculture pilot program (for beekeepers) use an index for different parts of the country.

Revenue-based policies:

Revenue Protection (RP) insures producers against yield losses due to natural causes such as drought, excessive moisture, hail, wind, frost, insects, and disease, and revenue losses caused by a change in the harvest price from the projected price. The producer selects the amount of average yield he or she wishes to insure, from 50% to 75% (in some areas to 85%). The projected price and the harvest price are 100% of the price determined by futures contracts. The amount of insurance protection is based on the greater of the projected price or the harvest price. If the harvested plus any appraised production multiplied by the harvest price is less than the amount of insurance protection, the producer is paid an indemnity based on the difference. The policy "Revenue Protection With Harvest Price Exclusion" is based on the projected price only (i.e., the amount of insurance protection is not increased if the harvest price is greater than the projected price).

Actual Revenue History (ARH) insures an average of historical grower revenues instead of insuring historical yields as done under APH. Like other revenue coverage plans, ARH protects growers against losses from low yields, low prices, low quality, or any combination of these events.

Area Revenue Protection (formerly Group Risk Income Protection or GRIP) makes indemnity payments only when the average county revenue for the insured crop falls below the revenue guarantee selected by the farmer; Area Revenue Protection with Harvest Price Exclusion is available if upside harvest price protection is not desired.

Whole-Farm Revenue Protection (WFRP) insures revenue of the entire farm rather than an individual crop by guaranteeing a portion of whole-farm historic average revenue (both crops and livestock). To calculate the guarantee, the plan uses five consecutive years of a producer's Schedule F tax form and current-year expected farm revenue. Beginning in 2015, it replaces Adjusted Gross Revenue (AGR) and AGR-Lite.

Livestock Policies insure against declining market prices or gross margins for swine, cattle, lambs, and milk.

III. Supplemental Coverage Option (SCO) may be purchased with CAT or Buy-up to cover part of the deductible of underlying policy. Eligible crops in 2015 are corn, cotton, sorghum, rice, soybeans, barley, and wheat.

Source: USDA's Risk Management Agency, http://www.rma.usda.gov/policies/.

Revenue-Based Insurance

Revenue insurance accounts for more than half of all crop insurance policies (*Figure 3*). It began in 1997 as a buy-up option on a pilot basis for major crops. By 2003, acreage under revenue-based insurance exceeded acreage covered by yield-based policies.[19]

A "Revenue Protection" policy combines the production guarantee component of crop insurance with a price guarantee to create a target revenue guarantee. Under revenue insurance programs, participating producers are assigned a target level of revenue based on expected market prices for the upcoming season and the producer's yield history. A farmer who opts for revenue insurance can receive an indemnity payment when his actual farm revenue (crop-specific or entire farm, depending on the policy) falls below a certain percentage of the target level of revenue, regardless of whether the shortfall is caused by low prices or low production levels. The price portion of the guarantee rises if the market strengthens between planting and harvest, unless the producer purchases "Revenue Protection With Harvest Price Exclusion." Insurable crops are barley, canola/rapeseed, corn, cotton, grain sorghum, peanuts, rice, soybeans, sunflowers, and wheat. For selected other crops such as tart cherries and strawberries, Actual Revenue History (ARH) insures historical revenues and protects growers against losses from low yields, low prices, low quality, or any combination of these events.

Whole Farm Revenue Protection (WFRP)

The Whole-Farm Revenue Protection (WFRP) policy insures revenue of the entire farm rather an individual crop. The policy is designed for highly diverse farms that are growing a wide range of commodities, including farms selling to local or regional, and farm-identity preserved, markets and growing specialty crops and animals and animal products. The amount of farm revenue that can be protected is the lower of the revenue expected on the current year's farm plan or five-year historic income adjusted for growth. All commodities produced by the farm are covered under WFRP except timber, forest, and forest products, and animals for sport, show or pets. Maximum total coverage per farm is $8.5 million.[20] WFRP replaces the Adjusted Gross Revenue (AGR) and AGR-Lite pilot programs and provides additional enhancements, such as a range of coverage levels from 50%-85% to fit the needs of more farming and ranching operations; replant coverage for annual crops; the ability to consider market readiness costs as part of the insured revenue and expenses; provisions to adjust the insurance guarantee to better fit expanding operations; and an improved timeline for operations that operate as fiscal year filers.

Crop Insurance Premium Subsidies

The producer's premium for a policy increases as coverage levels rise, and the premium on buy-up coverage is subsidized by the government at amounts from 38% to 100%, depending on the coverage level (*Table 1*). The subsidy rate declines as the coverage level rises (i.e., deductible declines).

Subsidy rates range from 38% to 67% for policies using either "basic" or "optional" units. Basic units cover all plantings in a single county of a crop with the same tenant/landlord. Optional units are basic units divided into smaller units by township section. As authorized under the 2008 farm bill, a higher subsidy rate (up to 80%) is provided for policies using enterprise units (all land for a single crop in a county, regardless of the tenant/landlord structure). Because the premium for policies using enterprise units is lower (a discount is given because the combined unit has greater geographic diversity and hence is less risky), a higher subsidy rate for enterprise units provides for an equal dollar amount of premium subsidy regardless of the type of unit used. Overall, the average subsidy rate across all policies purchased was 62% in 2014.

Table 1. Crop Insurance Premium Subsidies (government-paid portion of premium as a percent of total premium)

Coverage Level (%)	CAT	50	55	60	65	70	75	80	85
Premium subsidy (%) for most polices (including those using basic and optional units)	100	67	64	64	59	59	55	48	38
Premium subsidy (%) for enterprise units	n/a	80	80	80	80	80	77	68	53
Premium subsidy (%) for area plans (yield)	n/a	n/a	n/a	n/a	n/a	59	59	55	55
Premium subsidy (%) for area plans (revenue)	n/a	n/a	n/a	n/a	n/a	59	55	55	49
Premium subsidy (%) for whole farm units	n/a	80	80	80	80	80	80	71	56

Source: 7 U.S.C. §1508(e).

Notes: n/a = not applicable. A basic unit covers land in one county with the same tenant/landlord. An optional unit is a basic unit divided into smaller units by township section. An enterprise unit covers all land of a single crop in a county for a producer, regardless of tenant/landlord structure. A whole farm unit covers more than one crop. For CAT, a loss beyond 50% is indemnified at 55% of the expected price. For coverage level of 50%, a loss beyond that percentage is indemnified at a higher percentage of price (selected by the purchaser) within a minimum and maximum range set by RMA. Whole farm subsidy is for farms with three or more commodities; if commodity count is less than three, coverage is not available at 80% and 85%.

Geographic Distribution of Program Participation and Indemnities

With widespread use of crop insurance products for major crops (corn, cotton, soybeans, and wheat), the geographic distribution of acreage enrolled in crop insurance mirrors that of major producing areas (*Figure 4*). Crop insurance indemnities follow the same pattern, but with an emphasis on producing areas with less rainfall and more variable crop-weather conditions. For example, in 2011, relatively high indemnities were paid in the Great Plains, where drought reduced crop yields in the south and central areas while excessive moisture affected plantings and production in the north.[21] In 2012, a major drought affected a large portion of the United States, and crop insurance indemnities totaled $17.4 billion in 2012, compared with $10.9 billion in 2011 and $4.3 billion in 2010. With improved weather, indemnities declined to $12.1 billion in 2013 and $4.2 billion in 2014 (as of early December 2014). As was the case in 2013, losses in 2014 were extensive across the Plains due to continued drought conditions (*Figure 5*).

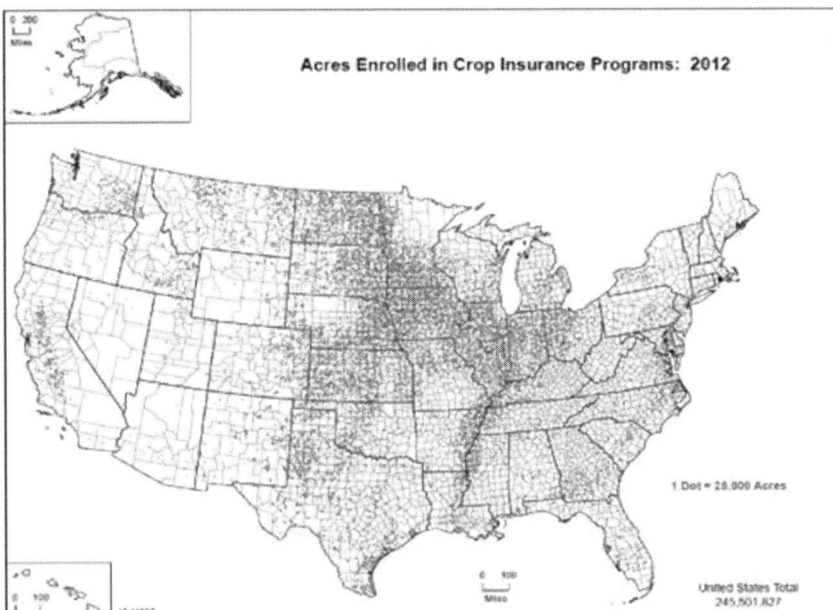

Source: USDA, National Agricultural Statistics Service, 2012 Census of Agriculture.

Figure 4. Acres Enrolled in Crop Insurance, 2012.

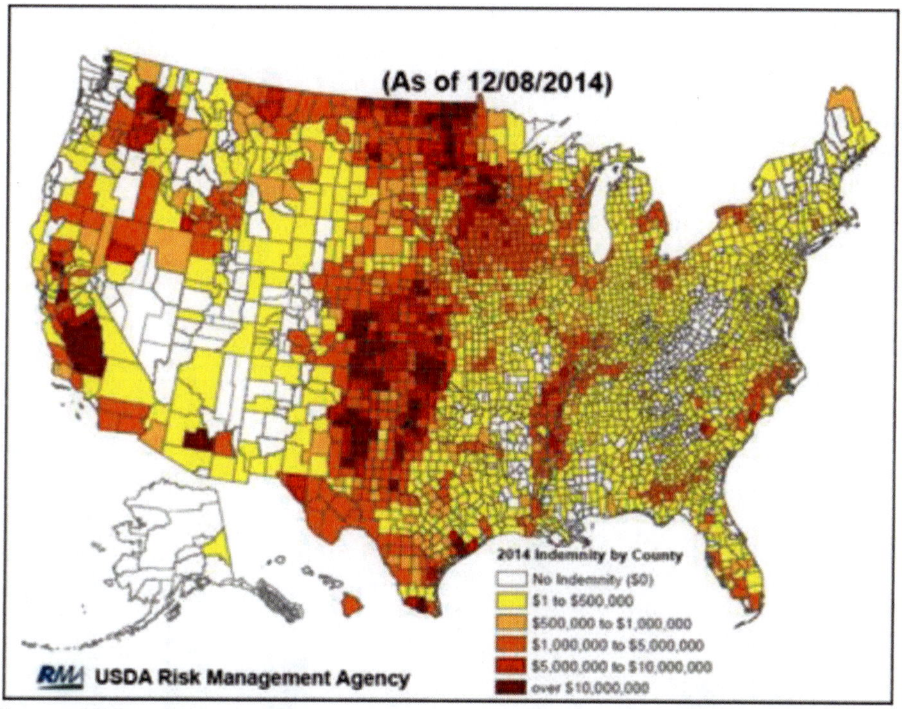

Source: USDA, Risk Management Agency, http://www.rma.usda.gov/data/indemnity/.

Figure 5. Crop Insurance Indemnities in 2014.

Distribution of Producer Subsidies

Producer subsidies for crop insurance are proportional to the value of the premiums and underlying liability of the policies. Compared with small farms, larger operations have greater crop liability, which increases the total costs of insurance and value of the government-paid portion of the total premium. Based on federal crop insurance expenditures data from USDA's Agricultural Resource Management Survey (ARMS) and the average subsidy percentage (62%) from RMA, CRS estimates that the producer subsidy in 2013 averaged about $19,000 per farm for farms purchasing crop insurance. By farm size, the calculated average ranged from $2,300 per farm for operations with less than $10,000 in sales to $115,000 for farms with at least $5 million in sales (see *Figure 6*). Unlike farm commodity programs, subsidies received under the crop insurance program are not subject to payment limits.

By crop, the bulk of producer subsidies are for corn, wheat, soybeans, and cotton, which together account for more than 80% of the premium subsidies (*Figure 7*). By state, premium subsidies are greatest in states where these crops are grown, primarily across the Great Plains, Corn Belt, and parts of the South (*Figure 8*). An analysis by the Government Accountability Office shows a similar geographic distribution for farmers receiving at least $40,000 in producer premium subsidies (*Figure 9*).

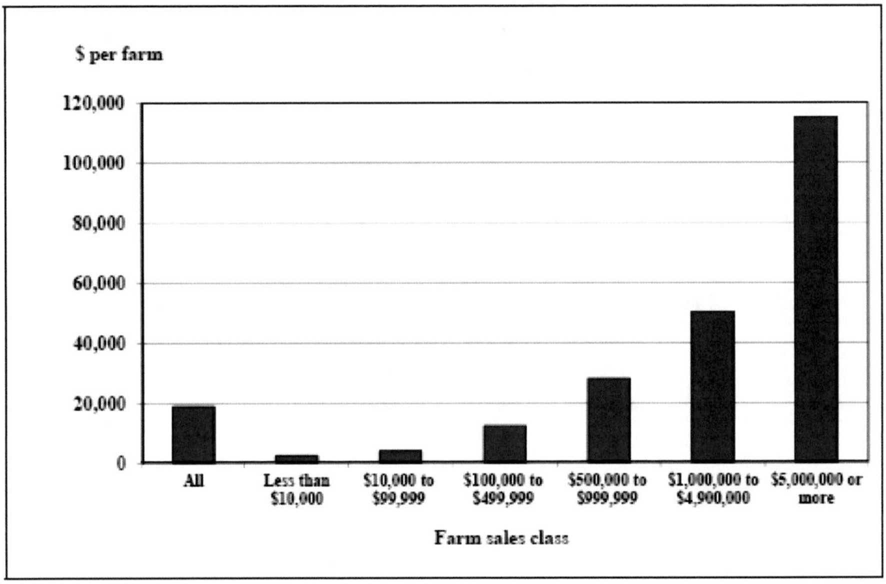

Source: CRS calculation using average premium subsidy of 62% from USDA's Risk Management Agency (RMA) and total federal crop insurance expenditures by farm sales class from USDA's Agricultural Resource Management Survey, provided by USDA's Economic Research Service.

Notes: The calculated average was $18,900 per farm (calculation includes only farms that pay federal crop insurance premiums). Total premium subsidy reported by RMA was $7.3 billion for crop year 2013.

Figure 6. Estimated Average Crop Insurance Premium Subsidy Per Farm in 2013.

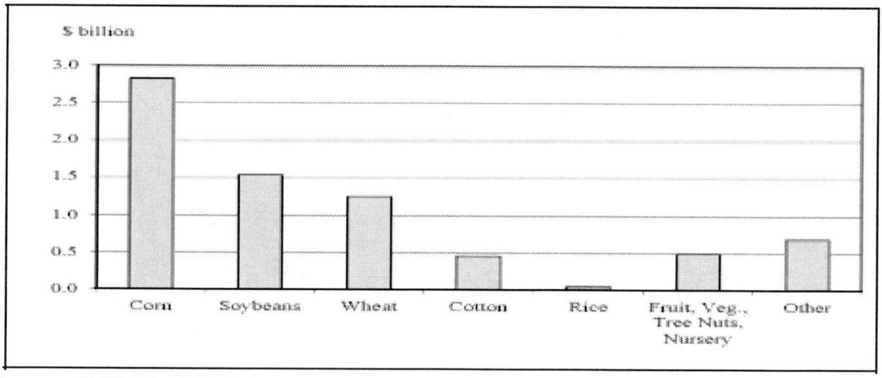

Source: USDA's Risk Management Agency, Summary of Business, http://www.rma.usda.gov/data/sob.html.

Notes: Total is $7.3 billion in crop year 2013. Corn, soybeans, wheat, and cotton account for 83% of the total.

Other includes minor oilseeds, other feed grains, tobacco, peanuts, sugar beets and sugar cane, pasture, and other crops.

Figure 7. Crop Insurance Premium Subsidies by Crop in 2013.

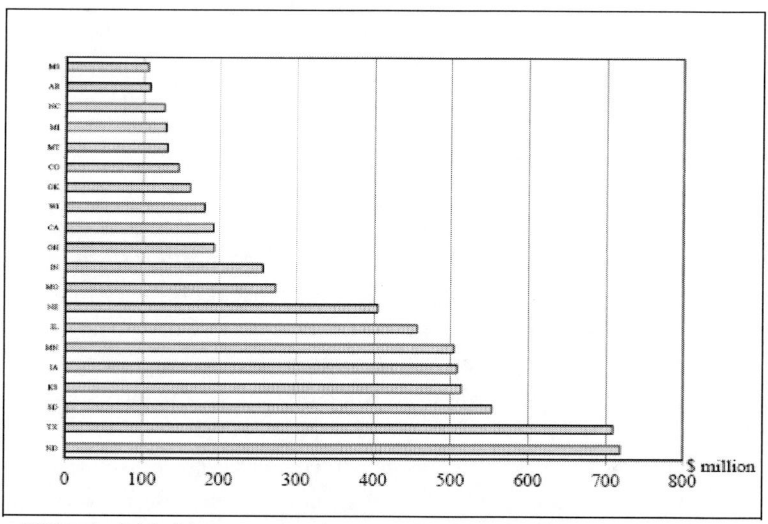

Source: USDA's Risk Management Agency, Summary of Business. http://www.rma.usda.gov/data/sob.html.

Notes: Total producer subsidy was $7.3 billion in crop year 2013. States in chart accounted for 87% of the total.

Figure 8. Crop Insurance Premium Subsidies for Top 20 States in 2013.

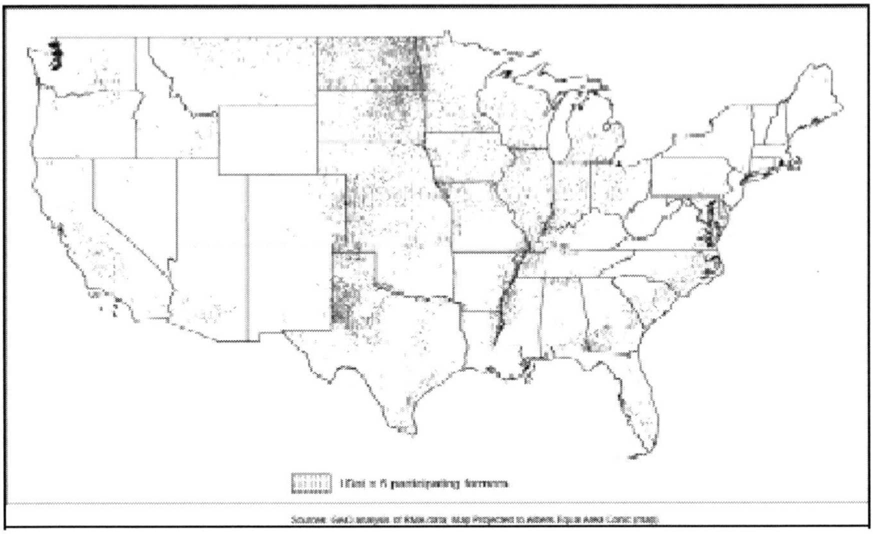

Source: U.S. Government Accountability Office, Crop Insurance: Savings Would Result from Program Changes and Greater Use of Data Mining, GAO-12-256, March 2012, p. 45, http://www.gao.gov/assets/590/589305.pdf.

Figure 9. Locations of Participating Farmers Receiving Premium Subsidies of More Than $40,000 in 2011.

FEDERAL PROGRAM COSTS

The annual agriculture appropriations bill traditionally makes two separate appropriations for the federal crop insurance program. It provides discretionary funding for the salaries and expenses of the RMA. It also provides "such sums as are necessary" for the Federal Crop Insurance Fund, which finances all other expenses of the program, including premium subsidies, indemnity payments, and reimbursements to the private insurance companies.

Government costs for crop insurance have increased substantially in the last decade (*Figure 10* and *Table 2*). After ranging between $2.1 billion and $3.9 billion during FY2000-FY2007, costs rose to $5.7 billion in FY2008 and $7.0 billion in FY2009 as higher policy premiums from rising crop prices drove up premium subsidies and expense reimbursements to private insurance companies. After a decline in FY2010 following a drop in crop prices and good weather, program costs rose sharply to $11.3 billion in FY2011 and

$14.1 billion in FY2012, when crop prices surged again and poor weather resulted in program losses. With a return to more favorable weather and smaller crop losses, total program costs declined to $6.0 billion in FY2013 and were $8.7 billion in FY2014.

The largest cost component of federal spending on crop insurance is for the subsidy on policy premiums for producers, which totaled $6.3 billion in FY2014. Historically, the next largest item is reimbursement of administrative and operating (A&O) expenses to private insurance companies ($1.4 billion in FY2014). With premiums reflecting only costs associated with policy risk, the A&O reimbursement is meant to pay delivery costs. In four of the last 10 years, the federal government also has realized underwriting losses (indemnities in excess of premiums received). In the other six years, the government has realized gains, which has partially reduced total costs. The underwriting gains (or losses) are derived in part from the federal government's role in providing the first level of reinsurance—that is, insurance for insurance companies.

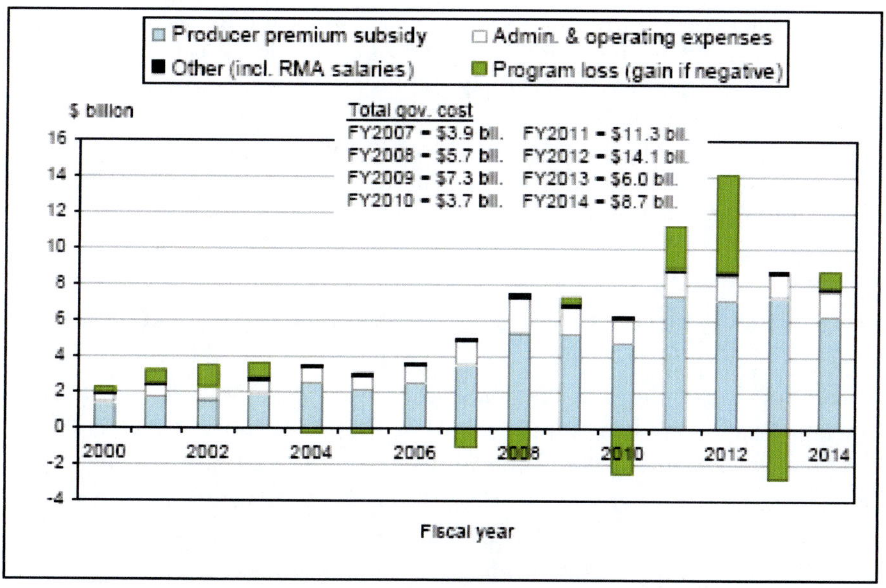

Source: CRS using data from U.S. Department of Agriculture, Risk Management Agency, http://www.rma.usda.gov/aboutrma/budget/costsoutlays.html.

Figure 10. Government Cost of Federal Crop Insurance.

Table 2. Government Cost of Federal Crop Insurance (millions of dollars)

Fiscal Year	Program Losses or (Gains)[a]	Federal Premium Subsidy	Private Company A&O Expense Reimbursements[b]	Other Costs[c]	Total Government Cost
2004	(305)	2,387	900	143	3,125
2005	(293)	2,070	783	139	2,699
2006	(32)	2,517	960	126	3,571
2007	(1,068)	3,544	1,341	124	3,941
2008	(1,717)	5,301	2,016	137	5,737
2009	340	5,198	1,602	131	7,271
2010	(2,523)	4,680	1,371	143	3,671
2011	2,392	7,376	1,383	144	11,295
2012	5,370	7,149	1,411	141	14,071
2013	(2,827)	7,279	1,350	149	5,951
2014 (est.)	847	6,272	1,407	133	8,659

Source: U.S. Department of Agriculture, Risk Management Agency, http://www.rma.usda.gov/aboutrma/budget/ costsoutlays.html.

[a] Government's underwriting loss (gain if negative) = the difference between total indemnity payments for crop losses and total premiums (farmer and government paid), plus or minus any private company underwriting gains or losses.

[b] A&O = administrative and operating.

[c] Other costs include federal salaries of USDA's RMA and, beginning in 2002, various research and development initiatives mandated by the Agriculture Risk Protection Act of 2000 (P.L. 106-224).

STANDARD REINSURANCE AGREEMENT (SRA)

The administrative and operating (A&O) expense reimbursement to the companies and risk sharing between USDA and the private companies are spelled out in a Standard Reinsurance Agreement (SRA), which plays a large role in determining program costs. The current SRA was completed in summer 2010. As authorized by the 2008 farm bill, USDA may renegotiate the SRA once every five years starting with the 2011 reinsurance year (the 12-month period beginning July 1, 2010). The 2014 farm bill requires that any renegotiated SRA must be budget-neutral, with the congressional intention that it not be used to cut federal funding of the crop insurance program.[22]

Administrative and Operating (A&O) Reimbursement

Under the current SRA, the calculated reimbursement rate for A&O has been approximately 12% of total premiums since 2011, compared with an average of 20% in 2006-2010.[23] This means that for every $100 in total premiums (farmer-paid plus government-paid), the companies receive a reimbursement of $12 from the federal government. The reimbursement rate varies by insurance product, depending on whether it is for a yield-based or a revenue insurance product.

The SRA places a maximum for A&O reimbursements at $1.3 billion per year (adjusted annually for inflation) and a minimum at $1.1 billion. The cap controls government costs when crop prices rise (price levels directly affect policy premiums), while the minimum is intended to protect companies against low market prices that could reduce reimbursement amounts.

Private Company Risk Sharing

The SRA also defines risk-sharing between the government and private insurance companies. Under the SRA, insurance companies may transfer some liability associated with riskier policies to the government and retain profits/losses from less risky policies.[24] This transfer of risk is accomplished through a set of reinsurance funds maintained by FCIC. Within 30 days of the sales closing dates for each crop, companies allocate each policy they sell to one of two funds that are maintained for each company by state: Assigned Risk or Commercial. Each company then decides what proportion of premiums (and potential for losses/gains) to retain within each reinsurance fund, subject to required retention limits of individual funds. The by-state retention requirements are 20% for the Assigned Risk Fund and at least 35% for the Commercial Fund. The ceded (i.e., not retained) portion of premiums goes to the government.

The assigned risk fund is used for policies believed to be high-risk because it provides the most loss protection to insurance companies through "stop-loss" coverage that reinsures against state-level disasters. For producers, it helps ensure that benefits of the federal crop insurance program are extended to all eligible farmers, regardless of risk. Because companies retain only 20% of their business as specified in the SRA, the federal government assumes a large portion of liability associated with high-risk policies. The SRA also specifies a 75% limit (by state) on the proportion of a company's business that may be placed in the Assigned Risk Fund.

The Commercial Fund is for policies that the companies expect to have the greatest opportunity for profit and only a small amount of losses. While the profit potential is greater compared with the Assigned Risk Fund, so is the loss potential.

Once the policies are allocated to one of the two funds, the gain/loss sharing for a company's retained business is based on loss ratios (indemnities paid divided by premiums collected) as established in the SRA. As a general rule, the higher the loss ratio, the lower the company share of gains or losses (and vice versa, except at very low loss ratios when the company share of gains declines). See *Table 3* for the schedule contained in the current SRA. *Figure 11* illustrates risk sharing for the Commercial Fund.

Table 3. Share of Crop Insurance Company's Gains/Losses by Fund and Loss Ratio (share of gains/losses in percent)

Loss Ratio (%)	Share of Company's Gains/Losses in Assigned Risk Fund (%)	Share of Company's Gains/Losses in Commercial Fund (%)	
		Group1 (IL, IN, IA, MN, NE)	All other states
0 to 50	3	5	5
>50 to 65	13.5	40	40
>65 to 100	22.5	75	97.5
>100 to 160	7.5	65	42.5
>160 to 220	6	45	20
>220 to 500	3	10	5
>500	0	0	0

Source: U.S. Department of Agriculture, Risk Management Agency, Standard Reinsurance Agreement dated June 30, 2010, http://www.rma.usda.gov/news/2010/06/630sra.pdf.

Notes: Loss ratio is indemnities divided by total premiums. See figure on risk sharing for illustration.

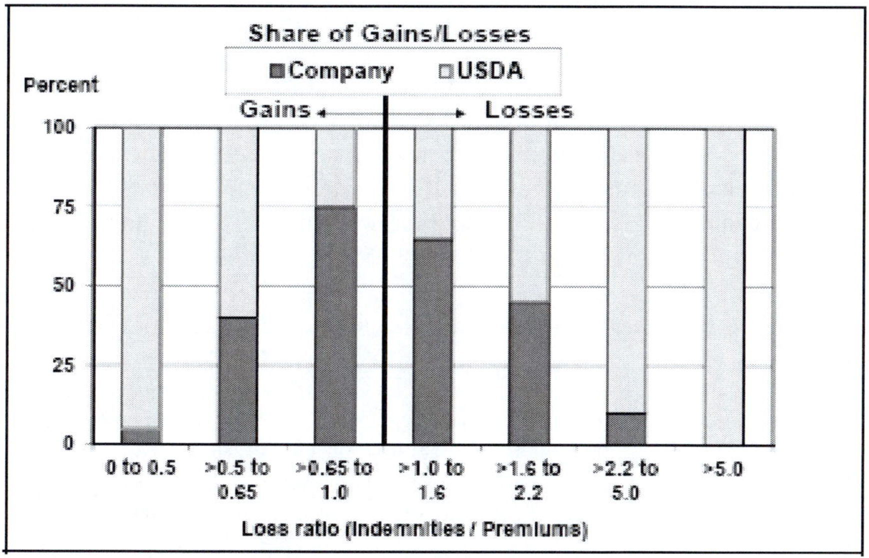

Source: CRS, using data from U.S. Department of Agriculture, Risk Management Agency, Standard Reinsurance Agreement dated June 30, 2010, http://www.rma.usda.gov/news/2010/06/630sra.pdf.

Notes: The USDA share of gains and losses is lowest when the loss ratio (indemnities divided by premiums) is near 1.0. Insurance companies place "less risky" policies in the Commercial Fund. Separate schedules apply to the Commercial Fund in all other states and for the Assigned Risk Fund (higher risk policies).

Figure 11. Risk Sharing for the Commercial Fund (for Group I states of IL, IN, IA, MN, NE).

Trends in A&O Reimbursement and Underwriting Gains

Since A&O reimbursements are based on a percentage of premiums, the dollar amount of A&O reimbursement increased sharply during the late 2000s as premiums rose, reflecting higher crop prices. The A&O reimbursement increased from an average of $881 million during 2004-2006 to $2.0 billion in 2008 (*Table 2*). A&O reimbursements declined to $1.6 billion in FY2009 following a decline in crop prices. Under changes in the 2010 SRA, an inflation-adjusted cap has limited annual A&O expenditures to about $1.4 billion. Company underwriting gains (the amount by which a company's share of retained premiums exceeds its indemnities) increased substantially during the 2000s as weather was generally favorable for crops (*Table 4*). In 2012, though, a major drought across major producing regions led to sharply higher indemnities, which resulted in large losses for the 2012 crop year. More favorable weather returned in 2013, which reduced indemnities and generated an underwriting gain for the insurance companies.

During the last decade, increases in insured acreage and higher crop prices have also increased gross liability. Liability represents total exposure of the program, meaning that if all participating farmers suffer losses to the full extent of coverage, indemnities would be the total liability.

Table 4. Federal Crop Insurance Program and Company Data

Crop Year	Net Acres Insured (mil. acres)	Gross Premium[a] ($ million)	Gross Liability[b] ($ million)	Gross Loss Ratio[c]	Private Co. Underwriting Gain (Loss)[d] ($ million)
2004	221	4,186	46,602	0.79	693
2005	246	3,949	44,259	0.60	915
2006	242	4,580	49,919	0.77	821
2007	272	6,562	67,340	0.54	1,577
2008	273	9,851	89,893	0.88	1,096
2009	265	8,951	79,572	0.58	2,301
2010	256	7,594	78,102	0.56	1,912
2011	266	11,970	114,201	0.91	1,687
2012	283	11,071	116,791	1.57	(1,299)
2013	296	11,805	123,775	1.02	657
2014 (est.)	294	10,043	109,664	not avail.	not avail.

Source: For premium, liability, and loss ratio, Summary of Business Report, FCIC, http://www.rma.usda.gov/data/ sob.html. For underwriting gain/loss, Crop Year Premium and Other Income, FCIC, http://www.rma.usda.gov/ aboutrma/budget/ 2014cyprem.pdf. Estimate for 2014 current as of January 2015.

[a] Farmer-paid premium plus government-paid premium subsidy.

[b] Liability represents total exposure of the program, meaning that if all participating farmers suffered losses to the full extent of coverage, program indemnities would be the total liability.

[c] Indemnities divided by premiums. Gross loss ratio is for the program in total (government plus private companies).

[d] The underwriting gains represent the amount by which the company's share of retained premiums exceeds its indemnities (vice versa for underwriting losses).

Crop Insurance in the 2014 Farm Bill

The federal crop insurance program is permanently authorized. Hence, periodic reauthorization of the program, including premium subsidies, is not needed, unlike farm commodity programs that are enacted under traditional "farm bills." The 2014 farm bill (P.L. 113-79) authorized farm programs for the years 2014-2018 and made a number of permanent changes to the federal crop insurance program.[25]

A prominent crop insurance feature of the 2014 farm bill is the authorization of policies designed to reimburse "shallow losses"—an insured producer's out-of-pocket loss associated with the policy deductible. A new crop insurance policy called Stacked Income Protection Plan (STAX) is made available for upland cotton producers, while the Supplemental Coverage Option (SCO) is made available for other crops. The STAX policy indemnifies losses in county revenue of greater than 10% of expected revenue but not more than the deductible level (e.g., 25%) selected by the producer for the underlying individual policy. (It can also be purchased as a stand-alone policy.) Similarly, SCO is based on expected county revenue (or yields) and covers part of the deductible under the producer's underlying policy. The government subsidy as a share of the policy premium is set at 80% for STAX and 65% for SCO.[26]

A variety of additional farm bill provisions expand existing crop insurance products or require examination of the potential for new products, including those that would benefit specialty crops and animal agriculture. Provisions revise the value of crop insurance for organic crops to reflect generally higher prices of organic (not conventional) crops. USDA is also required to conduct more research on whole farm revenue insurance with higher coverage levels than currently available. Studies or policies are also required for insuring (1) producers of specialty crops (e.g., fruits, vegetables) for food safety and contamination-related losses, (2) swine producers for a catastrophic disease event, (3) producers of catfish against reduction in the margin between market prices and production costs, (4) commercial poultry production against business disruptions caused by integrator bankruptcy, (5) poultry producers for a catastrophic event, (6) producers of biomass sorghum or sweet sorghum grown as feedstock for renewable energy, and (7) alfalfa producers. A peanut revenue insurance product and rice margin insurance also are mandated. Another provision provides funding for index weather insurance for protecting against weather conditions that deviate from average levels.

To address conservation concerns, the 2014 farm bill links eligibility for crop insurance premium subsidies to compliance with wetland and conservation requirements for highly erodible land. Also, crop insurance subsidies are reduced for plantings on native sod acreage in certain states.

Despite calls by critics of the program to reduce federal funding, the crop insurance title of the farm bill increased total funding for the program, according to the Congressional Budget Office, by an additional $5.7 billion over 10 years relative to projected levels that assumed no change in policy. The largest cost items were STAX ($3.3 billion) and SCO ($1.7 billion). The cost of expanding the crop insurance program was offset by the elimination of fixed "direct" payments, marking a policy shift from farm payments made regardless of market conditions to enhanced risk management programs. A controversial item not included in P.L. 113-79 was the reduction of premium subsidies for high-income farmers, which had been included in the Senate farm bill but not the House bill.

VIEWS ON FEDERAL CROP INSURANCE

Federal outlays for crop insurance exceed those for the commodity support programs, making crop insurance the most costly component of the farm safety net and a potential target for legislators looking for budget offsets to pay for other legislation or for deficit reduction. For some policy makers, a main goal when contemplating future modifications to the crop insurance program would likely be saving federal dollars without adversely affecting farmer participation or policy coverage in a way that might result in calls for ad hoc disaster assistance. A concern from the industry is that any cuts could adversely affect company interest in selling and servicing crop insurance to farmers, although some critics say that compensation is more than adequate. Separately, environmental groups are concerned that the premium subsidies might actually encourage production on environmentally fragile land.

For many farmers, crop insurance is the most important component of the farm safety net, given the loss protection it affords and the large number of crops that are covered. Similarly, institutions that lend to farmers support federal crop insurance because it helps buffer cash shortfalls. Another major supporter is the set of approved insurance providers and the network of independent agents who sell and service the federal policies. With significant support from these three groups, the program generally has widespread support among farm-state legislators and Members of the agriculture committees where farm policy is developed.

During the debate that shaped the 2014 farm bill, critics of crop insurance vigorously attempted but were not successful in reducing the scope and benefits of the federal crop insurance program, including premium subsidy levels and reimbursements to private insurance companies. Critics question whether premium subsidies are too generous for farmers, particularly high-income farmers, and expect that farmers would maintain crop insurance coverage at lower subsidy rates. The issue of program savings might be revisited in the 114th Congress, particularly if future budget resolutions require deficit reduction.

End Notes

[1] For more on the history of federal crop insurance, see http://www.rma.usda.gov/aboutrma/what/history.html. Law citations are the Federal Crop Insurance Act of 1980 (P.L. 96-365), the Federal Crop Insurance Reform Act of 1994 (P.L. 103-354), and the Agriculture Risk Protection Act (ARPA) of 2000 (P.L. 106-224). Additional background on the program's rationale is available the following three articles: (1) Joseph W. Glauber, "The Growth of the Federal Crop Insurance Program, 1990-2011," Amer. J. Agr. Econ., vol. 95, no. 2 (January 2013), pp. 482-488; (2) Keith H. Coble and Barry J. Barnett, "Why Do We Subsidize Crop Insurance?," Amer. J. Agr. Econ., vol. 95, no. 2 (January 2013), pp. 498-504; and (3) Barry K. Goodwin and Vincent H, Smith, "What Harm Is Done by Subsidizing Crop Insurance?," Amer. J. Agr. Econ., vol. 95, no. 2 (January 2013), pp. 489-497.

[2] CRS Report R43494, Crop Insurance Provisions in the 2014 Farm Bill (P.L. 113-79).

[3] In practice, the crop insurance company bills the farmer for the producer's portion of the premium (i.e., excluding the government portion). The company then sends the entire producer-paid premium to RMA. When a producer files a claim and the company pays an indemnity, RMA reimburses the company in full for the loss. At the end of the reinsurance year, there is an annual settlement whereby the company's proportion of any underwriting gain or loss is determined and paid.

[4] Insured percentage is for 2011. For a detailed analysis by crop, see USDA Risk Management Agency, The Risk Management Safety Net: Portfolio Analysis-Market Penetration and Potential, Washington, DC, August 2013, http://www.rma.usda.gov/pubs/2013/ portfolio/portfolio.pdf.

[5] A complete list of 2015 crops is available at http://www.rma.usda.gov/policies/ 2015 policy.html.

[6] Carey Frick, "Frick: Not So Peachy," The State, May 26, 2010.

[7] USDA Risk Management Agency, The Risk Management Safety Net: Portfolio Analysis-Market Penetration and Potential, Washington, DC, August 2013, http://www.rma.usda.gov/pubs/2013/portfolio/portfolio.pdf. For additional information, see Federal Crop Insurance Corporation, Report to Congress: Specialty Crop Report, Washington, DC, November 2010, http://www.rma.usda.gov/pubs/2010/specialtycrop.pdf.

[8] For descriptions of Livestock Gross Margin (margin protection) and Livestock Risk Protection (price protection), see http://www.rma.usda.gov/livestock/.

[9] For more information, see http://www.rma.usda.gov/policies/pasturerangeforage/. Also see Monte Vandeveer, Pasture, Rangeland, and Forage Insurance: A Risk Management Tool for Hay and Livestock Producers, University of Nebraska-Lincoln, October 2012, http://cropwatch.unl.edu/c/document_library/get_file?uuid=3f25e3ef-68d1-4489-a7dd-7daba3c2d385&groupId=1841&.pdf.

[10] For a description of the program, see http://www.rma.usda.gov/policies/ri-vi/annual forage.html.

[11] A list of RMA regional offices is available at http://www.rma.usda.gov/ aboutrma/fields/ rsos.html.

[12] For more information, see USDA, Risk Management Agency, Requesting Insurance Not Available in Your County, Program Aid 1929, September 2013, http://www.rma.usda.gov/pubs/rme/requestinginsurance.pdf. See also the FCIC "Written Agreement Handbook," http://www.rma.usda.gov/handbooks/24000/2013/24020.pdf.

[13] For more information on NAP, see the USDA fact sheet at http://fsa.usda.gov/Internet/FSA_File/nap09.pdf.

[14] Growers have expressed a preference for no development of insurance products for a number of crops; see Attachment 2 in USDA Risk Management Agency, The Risk Management Safety Net: Portfolio Analysis-Market Penetration and Potential, Washington, DC, August 2013, http://www.rma.usda.gov/pubs/2013/portfolio/portfolio.pdf.

[15] U.S. Department of Agriculture, Risk Management Agency, http://www.rma.usda.gov/help/faq/basics.html.

[16] For a detailed discussion, see U.S. Department of Agriculture, Risk Management Agency, Premium Rate Adjustment, November 2012, http://www.rma.usda.gov/news/2012/11/2013 premiumrateadjustment.pdf.

[17] A number of university and Extension Service offices provide information to farmers when making crop insurance decisions. Some examples include http://www.agmanager.info/crops/insurance/risk_mgt/default.asp, http://www.ag.ndsu.nodak.edu/ aginfo/cropmkt/cic.htm, and http://www.farmdoc.uiuc.edu/cropins/index.asp.

[18] Participation at the CAT level has steadily decreased, particularly since subsidies on buy-up levels were increased in the Agriculture Risk Protection Act (ARPA) of 2000. In 2014, only about 5% of insured acres were insured at the CAT level.

[19] After years of development, USDA's Risk Management Agency issued the "COMBO" rule in late March 2010 to consolidate several crop insurance plans into a single "Common Crop Insurance Policy" beginning with the 2011 crop year. The biggest change was the consolidation of several previous revenue products (Crop Revenue Coverage, Income Protection, Indexed Income Protection, and Revenue Assurance) into a single revenue product called Revenue Protection. See USDA, Risk Management Agency, "RMA Releases New Common Crop Insurance Policy Basic Provisions," press release, March 31, 2010, http://www.rma.usda.gov/news/2010/03/combo.html.

[20] Additional information on WFRP is available from USDA/RMA at http://www.rma.usda.gov/policies/wfrp.html.

[21] Adverse weather can affect crops in various ways. For example, in some North Dakota counties in 2009, the cause of loss was drought for some wheat policies, while it was excess moisture for other wheat policies in the same county.

[22] For more information on the SRA and related issues, see CRS Report R40966, Renegotiation of the Standard Reinsurance Agreement (SRA) for Federal Crop Insurance.

[23] The lower calculated rate is a result of a significant rise in premiums between the two periods and legislative changes. The 2008 farm bill (§12016(E)) reduced the A&O reimbursement

by 2.3 percentage points beginning with the 2009 reinsurance year (July 1, 2008). The farm bill also reduced the A&O reimbursement rate to 12% for any plan of insurance that is based on area-wide losses and reduced the target loss ratio (indemnities paid divided by premiums collected of the entire program) from 1.075 to 1.00.

[24] Dmitry V. Vedenov et al., "Portfolio Allocation and Alternative Structures of the Standard Reinsurance Agreement," vol. 31, no. 1 (April 2006), pp. 57-73, http://ageconsearch.umn.edu/bitstream/10145/1/31010057.pdf. See also Joseph W. Glauber, "Crop Insurance Reconsidered," American Journal of Agricultural Economics, vol. 86, no. 5 (2004), pp. 1179-1195.

[25] For more information, see CRS Report R43494, Crop Insurance Provisions in the 2014 Farm Bill (P.L. 113-79).

[26] Additional information and examples of SCO and STAX are available in USDA, FCIC, Supplemental Coverage Option (SCO) Endorsement Standards Handbook, July 2014, http://www.rma.usda.gov/handbooks/18000/2015/ 15_18180.pdf; and Stacked Income Protection Plan of Insurance (STAX) Standards Handbook, August 2014, http://www.rma.usda.gov/handbooks/18000/2015/15_18170.pdf.

In: Federal Crop Insurance
Editor: Audrey Pope

ISBN: 978-1-63483-366-0

Chapter 2

CROP INSURANCE: IN AREAS WITH HIGHER CROP PRODUCTION RISKS, COSTS ARE GREATER, AND PREMIUMS MAY NOT COVER EXPECTED LOSSES*

United States Government Accountability Office

ABBREVIATIONS

APH	actual production history
ASB	Actuarial Standards Board
CBO	Congressional Budget Office
OIG	Office of Inspector General
RMA	Risk Management Agency
USDA	U. S. Department of Agriculture

WHY GAO DID THIS STUDY

The federally subsidized crop insurance program, which helps farmers manage the risk inherent in farming, has become one of the most important

* This is an edited, reformatted and augmented version of a report, GAO-15-215, issued by the Government Accountability Office, dated February 2015.

programs in the farm safety net. Since 2000, the government's costs for the crop insurance program have increased substantially. The program's cost has come under scrutiny as the nation's budgetary pressures have been increasing.

GAO was asked to identify the costs to the federal government for insuring crops in areas with higher production risks. This report examines, for these areas, (1) the government's cost of the crop insurance program and (2) the extent to which RMA's premium rates, as implemented, cover expected losses. GAO analyzed RMA crop insurance program data from 1994 through 2013 (the most recent year with complete program data) and premium rate data for 2013 and 2014; reviewed relevant studies, RMA documents, and documents from stakeholders including farm industry groups; and interviewed RMA officials.

What GAO Recommends

GAO recommends that RMA (1) monitor and report on crop insurance costs in areas that have higher crop production risks and (2), as appropriate, increase its adjustments of premium rates in these areas by as much as the full 20 percent annually that is allowed by law.

RMA disagreed with GAO's first recommendation and agreed with the second. GAO continues to believe that RMA can and should do more to monitor and report on crop insurance costs in higher risk areas, where government costs were found to be substantially higher.

What GAO Found

The federal government's crop insurance costs are substantially higher in areas with higher crop production risks (e.g., drought risk) than in other areas. In the higher risk areas, government costs per dollar of crop value for 2005 through 2013 were over two and a half times the costs in other areas. However, the U.S. Department of Agriculture's (USDA) Risk Management Agency (RMA)—the agency that administers the crop insurance program—does not monitor and report on the government's crop insurance costs in the higher risk areas.

RMA implemented changes to premium rates in 2014, decreasing some rates and increasing others, but GAO's analysis of RMA data shows that, for some crops, RMA's higher risk premium rates may not cover expected losses. RMA made changes to premium rates from 2013 to 2014, but its plans to phase in changes to premium rates over time could have implications for improving actuarial soundness. USDA is required by statute to limit annual increases in premium rates to 20 percent of what the farmer paid for the same coverage in the previous year. However, GAO found that, for higher risk premium rates that required an increase of at least 20 percent to cover expected losses, RMA did not raise these premium rates as high as the law allows to make the rates more actuarially sound. Without sufficient increases to premium rates, where applicable, RMA may not fully cover expected losses and make the rates more actuarially sound. Furthermore, in analyzing data on premium dollars for 2013, GAO found that had RMA's higher risk premium rates been more actuarially sound, the federal government could have potentially collected tens of millions of dollars in additional premiums.

* * *

February 9, 2015

The Honorable Ron Johnson
Chairman
Committee on Homeland Security and Governmental Affairs
United States Senate

The Honorable James Lankford
Chairman
Subcommittee on Regulatory Affairs and Federal Management
Committee on Homeland Security and Governmental Affairs
United States Senate

The federally subsidized crop insurance program, which helps farmers manage the risk inherent in farming, has become one of the most important programs in the farm safety net. Farmers can insure against losses caused by poor crop yields resulting from natural causes, declines in crop prices, or both, for each insurable crop they produce. The U.S. Department of Agriculture's (USDA) Risk Management Agency (RMA) has overall responsibility for administering the crop insurance program, including controlling costs. Currently, RMA partners with 19 private insurance companies that sell and service the insurance policies and share a percentage of the risk of loss and opportunity for gain associated with each policy. The federal government pays for (1) part of farmers' crop insurance premiums, which averaged about 62 percent of total premiums in 2013, and (2) administrative and operating expenses of insurance companies to cover their expenses for selling and servicing crop insurance policies.

Since 2000, the government's costs for the federal crop insurance program have increased substantially. Federal costs for the program averaged $3.4 billion annually for fiscal years 2003 through 2007 and grew to an average of $8.4 billion annually for fiscal years 2008 through 2013. The Congressional Budget Office (CBO) estimates that federal crop insurance costs will average $8.9 billion per year for fiscal years 2015 through 2024.[1] The cost of the federal crop insurance program has come under scrutiny as the nation's budgetary pressures have been increasing. In an October 2013 review of the federal government's long-term fiscal outlook, we concluded that current fiscal policy is unsustainable over the long term and that addressing the fiscal challenges of the future will require looking at the entire range of federal activities and making difficult choices in setting priorities.[2]

Budget pressures have been increasing in recent years and, at the same time, net farm income reached historically high levels. According to USDA's Economic Research Service (ERS), a primary source of economic information and research, net farm income is forecast to be $96.9 billion in 2014, down 23.4 percent from 2013's forecast of $126.5 billion. If realized, according to ERS, the 2014 amount would be the lowest since 2010, but net farm income would still be more than $14.5 billion higher than ERS' previous 10-year annual average (2004 through 2013).

In 2012 and 2013 reports, we suggested that Congress reduce crop insurance costs by limiting the amount of premium subsidies that an individual farmer can receive each year, reducing premium subsidy rates for all farmers, or by some combination of limiting and reducing these subsidies.[3] The Senate approved farm legislation in 2013 that would have reduced premium subsidies for some farmers, but this provision was not included in the final 2014 farm bill. In March 2014, the President's fiscal year 2015 budget proposed reductions in some premium subsidy rates. In August 2014, we suggested that Congress consider reducing the level of federal premium subsidies for revenue crop insurance policies.[4]

Crop insurance premium subsidies contribute to relatively high government costs in areas of the country with higher crop production risks—that is, areas that have higher risks of crop losses from drought, excessive moisture, or other natural causes. Because premiums are typically higher for policies covering crops in these areas, and premium subsidies are set at fixed percentages of the premiums, the premium subsidies are also higher.

Current law directs RMA to adopt premium rates and coverage levels that improve the actuarial soundness of the federal crop insurance program.[5] As a result, according to RMA, it must set premium rates and implement changes to premium rates in a timely manner to cover expected losses and allow for a reasonable reserve.[6] Current law also directs RMA to conduct periodic reviews of premium rates, including the methodology the agency uses for establishing premium rates.[7] RMA conducted its most recent study of its methodology for setting premium rates in 2010. Among other things, the study authors found that RMA's methodology was sound, but that the underlying data should be revised. Specifically, they concluded that the agency should place more weight on loss experience from more recent years to better account for current risks faced by farmers.[8] RMA adopted findings from the study, and a revision of its methodology necessitated a change in premium rates. RMA is directed by statute to implement new rates in a timely manner in order to improve actuarial soundness. According to an RMA document, this provision ensures that the federal crop insurance program does not place an unnecessary financial burden on farmers or the government through inaccurate premium rates.

In this context, you asked us to identify the costs to the federal government for insuring crops in areas with higher production risks in comparison with costs for insuring the same crops in areas with relatively lower production risks.[9] Our objectives were to determine, for areas with higher crop production risks, (1) the government's cost of the crop insurance program and (2) the extent to which RMA's premium rates, as implemented, cover expected losses.

To address these objectives, we reviewed relevant provisions of the Food, Conservation, and Energy Act of 2008 (2008 farm bill) and the Agricultural Act of 2014 (2014 farm bill); other statutes; and USDA regulations. To address the first objective, we analyzed RMA crop insurance program data for the crop years 1994 through 2013, for the five major crops—corn, soybeans, wheat, cotton, and grain sorghum.[10] To identify areas with higher production risks, we used 2013 county target premium rates—that is, the premium rates that RMA determines for each county and each crop based on the county's loss history.[11] We calculated a weighted average county target premium rate for each county in 2013 combining the county target premium rates for all five crops (and all of the crops' practices and crop types) using 2013 premium dollars. We then ranked the counties' weighted average county target premium rates from the highest to the lowest. We considered the 20 percent of counties that had the highest weighted average county target premium rates to have the highest crop production risks (or, "higher risk counties") and the remaining 80 percent to have the lowest crop production risks (or, "lower risk counties").[12] To calculate total government costs in these higher risk counties, we analyzed RMA data.[13] We also interviewed RMA officials regarding the RMA regional offices' role in monitoring premium rates. In addition, we reviewed USDA's and other studies that examined the costs of the crop insurance program and the role of premium subsidies and reviewed documents from other stakeholders, including farm industry groups. To address the second objective, we analyzed RMA data on county premium rates for the five major crops, for crop years 2013 and 2014.[14] We also interviewed RMA officials in headquarters and two field offices—selected based on their experience administering policies in areas with higher production risks—regarding the agency's method for setting and implementing changes to county premium rates. In addition, we reviewed USDA's and other studies that examined the agency's methodology for assigning premium rates and reviewed relevant audits by USDA's Office of the Inspector General. To evaluate the reliability of all of the RMA data, we reviewed related documentation, interviewed knowledgeable agency officials, and reviewed related internal controls information. In each case, we concluded that the data were sufficiently reliable for the purposes of this report. A more detailed discussion of our objectives, scope, and methodology is presented in appendix I.

We conducted this performance audit from December 2013 to February 2015 in accordance with generally accepted government auditing standards. Those standards require that we plan and perform the audit to obtain sufficient, appropriate evidence to provide a reasonable basis for our findings and conclusions based on our audit objectives. We believe that the evidence obtained provides a reasonable basis for our findings and conclusions based on our audit objectives.

BACKGROUND

The authorizing legislation for the federal crop insurance program states that the purpose of the program is to promote the national welfare by improving the economic stability of agriculture.[15] According to RMA's mission statement, the agency provides risk-management tools, such as crop insurance, to strengthen the economic stability of agricultural producers and rural communities. Specifically, RMA's fiscal years 2011 to 2015 strategic plan states that the agency's goal for the federal crop insurance program is that it will provide a broad-based financial safety net for producers. The fiscal years 2011 to 2015 strategic plan includes the agency's strategic goals and core values in support of its mission. These goals are, among other things, to continue to expand participation, ensure actuarially sound products, safeguard the integrity of the program, and to do so as responsible stewards of taxpayer dollars and with transparency.

Through the federal crop insurance program, farmers insure against losses on more than 100 crops. These crops include the five major crops (corn, soybeans, wheat, cotton, and grain sorghum), as well as nursery crops and certain fruits and vegetables. According to an RMA document, the amount of federal crop insurance purchased based on planted acres is relatively high in comparison with the past for the five major crops. In 2012, corn acreage was 84 percent insured, soybean acreage was 84 percent insured, wheat acreage was 83 percent insured, cotton acreage was 94 percent insured, and grain sorghum acreage was 74 percent insured.

As shown in table 1, the federal government's crop insurance costs generally increased for fiscal years 2003 through 2013. A widespread drought and crop losses in crop year 2012 contributed to the spike in government costs to $14.1 billion in fiscal year 2012.[16] In crop year 2013, weather conditions were more favorable, so government costs were lower than in fiscal year 2012. According to an April 2014 CBO estimate, for fiscal years 2014 through 2023, program costs are expected to average $8.9 billion annually.

RMA charges premiums to farmers to cover the risk of insuring crops against expected crop losses. RMA calculates premiums by multiplying the value of the insured crop, a base premium rate, and adjustment factors, which individualize the premium rate to a farmer's particular crop, yield history, geographic dispersion of the lands insured, and the percentage of the crop value that the farmer chooses to insure. Premium rates vary by crop, practice (e.g., irrigated or nonirrigated), type (e.g., spring wheat or winter wheat), and location (i.e., county).

RMA distinguishes between "base" premium rates and "target" premium rates. RMA sets a "base" and "target" premium rate for each county. In this report, we refer to this base premium rate as the *county base premium rate* and the target premium rate as the *county target premium rate.*

The *county base premium rate* is the rate upon which a farmer's individual premium rate is based.[17] The county base premium rate reflects past loss experience.

Table 1. Government Cost of Federal Crop Insurance, Fiscal Years 2003 through 2013

Fiscal year	Premiums and other income[a]	Loss claim payments	Loss claims paid in excess of premiums and other income	Premium subsidies	Administrative expenses	Other costs	Total government costs
2003	$2,946	$3,768	$822	$1,874	$743	$149	$3,588
2004	3,133	2,828	(305)	2,387	900	143	3,125
2005	3,089	2,796	(293)	2,070	783	139	2,699
2006	3,617	3,585	(32)	2,517	960	126	3,571
2007	4,561	3,493	(1,068)	3,544	1,341	124	3,941
2008	6,741	5,024	(1,717)	5,301	2,016	137	5,737
2009	8,076	8,416	340	5,198	1,602	131	7,271
2010	5,282	2,759	(2,523)	4,680	1,371	143	3,671
2011	11,037	13,429	2,392	7,376	1,383	144	11,295
2012	13,058	18,428	5,370	7,149	1,411	141	14,071
2013	$8,985	$6,158	($2,827)	$7,279	$1,350	$149	$5,951

Source: GAO analysis of USDA's Risk Management Agency (RMA) data. | GAO-15-215.

Note: According to an RMA document, total government costs are equal to loss claim payments to farmers minus premiums and other income received by the government plus premium subsidies provided on behalf of farmers plus administrative and operating expenses paid to insurance companies plus other costs.

[a] Premiums and other income are equal to premiums paid by farmers plus premium subsidies plus interest and other income minus underwriting gain (or plus underwriting loss).

As RMA accumulates information about new loss experience, it incorporates that information into the *county base premium rate*. Generally, a high county base premium rate indicates a high past crop loss history, and a lower county base premium rate suggests the opposite. The *county target premium rate* is the rate that RMA estimates to be the actuarially sound premium rate. RMA calculates the county base premium rate for each crop in each county by averaging the crop loss history over the preceding 20-year period and adjusting the rate to a standardized coverage level, which RMA sets at the 65 percent coverage level. The county target premium rate is the rate RMA sets as the benchmark for the county base premium rate.

The county base premium rate is the premium rate that is charged to a farmer, and the county target premium rate is the premium rate that RMA would need to charge farmers to fully cover expected losses. To fully cover expected losses, the county base premium rate should equal the county target premium rate. However, the county base premium rate can, over time, become out of alignment so that it is less than or greater than the county target premium rate. The county base premium rate may differ from the county target premium rate because changes in the rates due to actual loss history may outpace RMA's ability to increase or decrease rates due to statutory limitations and RMA's practices for adjusting rates.[18] In addition to conducting required reviews of its methodology for determining premium rates, RMA conducts periodic reviews of county base premium rates and county target premium rates based on new information about county losses.[19]

The federal government's premium subsidies for crop insurance policies are not actual monetary payments to farmers, but they can be considered a financial benefit to farmers. Without a premium subsidy, a participating farmer would have to pay more because he would be responsible for the full amount of the policy premium. Congress sets premium subsidy rates, meaning the percentage of the premium paid by the government. Premium subsidy rates vary by the level of insurance coverage that the farmer chooses.[20] For most policies, the statutory premium subsidy rates range from 38 percent to 80 percent. Premium subsidy rates increased, as a percentage of total premiums, from an average of 37 percent in 2000 to an average of 62 percent in 2013. In addition, premium subsidies rose as crop prices increased because higher prices meant the insured value of the crop increased, and premiums are based on the value of what is insured.

The federal government provides crop insurance premium subsidies in part to achieve high crop insurance participation and coverage levels. 21 Higher participation and coverage levels may reduce or eliminate the need for disaster assistance payments from congressionally authorized ad hoc disaster programs to help farmers recover from natural disasters, which can be costly. A 2005 USDA publication[22] asserts that Congress passed the Federal Crop Insurance Act of 1980 and subsequent related legislation to strengthen participation in the crop insurance program with the goal of replacing costly disaster assistance programs. According to this publication, the government has historically attempted to increase participation in the federal crop insurance program by subsidizing premiums, including increasing the level of these subsidies over time. In 2012, a major drought occurred, but Congress did not authorize ad hoc disaster payments. According to several farm groups, there were no calls for ad hoc disaster assistance in 2012 because of the protection crop insurance provided. Another possible reason was that, according to a 2013 Congressional Research Service report, under budget rules, the cost of ad hoc disaster payments would have to have been offset by spending cuts elsewhere.

The 2014 farm bill included a provision that affects the dollar value that a farmer can insure when the farmer's county has experienced substantial crop losses in previous years. RMA uses the actual production history (APH)—4 to 10 years of historical crop yields— to establish a farmer's insurance guarantee. Existing law before the 2014 farm bill allowed a farmer to replace a low actual yield in the APH with a yield equal to 60 percent of the historical county crop yield. The 2014 farm bill enhanced this provision by allowing farmers to exclude without replacement any recorded or appraised yield from the APH calculation if the average crop yield in the county for any particular year is less than 50 percent of the 10-year county average. According to a USDA document, this provision will provide relief to farmers affected by severe weather, including drought, by allowing them to have a higher approved crop yield. In general, RMA will set increased premium rates for farmers who choose to use this option, meaning the subsidy provided by the federal government will increase. CBO estimated that this provision change will cost $357 million over the 10 years from fiscal year 2014 through fiscal year 2023.

THE GOVERNMENT'S CROP INSURANCE COSTS ARE GREATER IN AREAS WITH HIGHER CROP PRODUCTION RISKS

The government's crop insurance costs are substantially higher in areas with higher crop production risks than in other areas. From 2005 through 2013, government costs per dollar of crop value in areas with higher crop production risks were over two and a half times the costs in other areas. However, RMA does not monitor and report on the government's crop insurance costs in these higher risk areas.

According to an RMA official, RMA's county target premium rates are the best available measure of crop production risks. In the 20 percent (510) of U.S. counties with the highest average county target premium rates, these rates ranged from 20 percent to 83 percent, with a median rate of 25 percent.[23] In comparison with other types of property and casualty insurance, 25 percent is a relatively high premium rate. For example, at 25 percent, the annual homeowner's insurance premium on a house valued at $400,000 would be $100,000. The remaining 80 percent (2,044) of U.S. counties had lower average county target premium rates. Those rates ranged from 0.6 percent to nearly 20 percent, with the median rate of 9 percent.

Figure 1 shows counties organized in groups of 20 percent based on average county target premium rates, with the darker areas representing counties with higher average county target premium rates. The color-shaded counties represent all 2,554 counties that had county target premium rates for at least one of the five major crops.

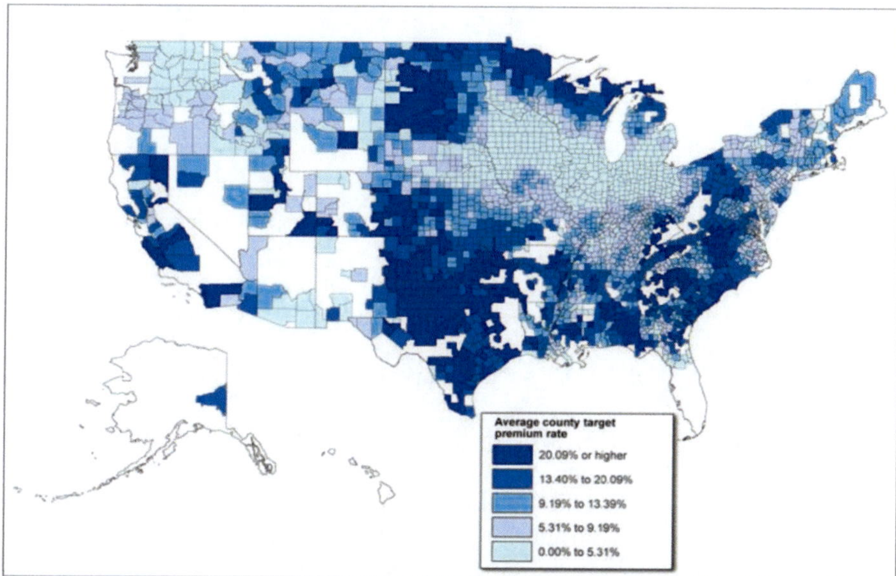

Source: GAO analysis of USDA's Risk Management Agency crop insurance data: MapInfo (map). | GAO-15-215.

Note: To identify areas with higher crop production risks, we determined the average of each county's 2013 county target premium rates for the five major crops—corn, soybeans, wheat, cotton, and grain sorghum. These averages were weighted by crop, crop type, and practice based on county premium dollars. The white areas on the map represent counties that did not have target rates for any of these crops.

Figure 1. Average County Target Premium Rates for the Federal Crop Insurance Program by Groups of 20 Percent, 2013.

Figure 2 shows the riskiest 20 percent of counties (510) in terms of average county target premium rates.[24] These 510 higher risk counties are color-shaded on the basis of their 2013 premium dollars to show which counties purchased the most crop insurance. The Great Plains, which has areas with relatively high drought risk, had a large portion of the higher risk counties' premium dollars.

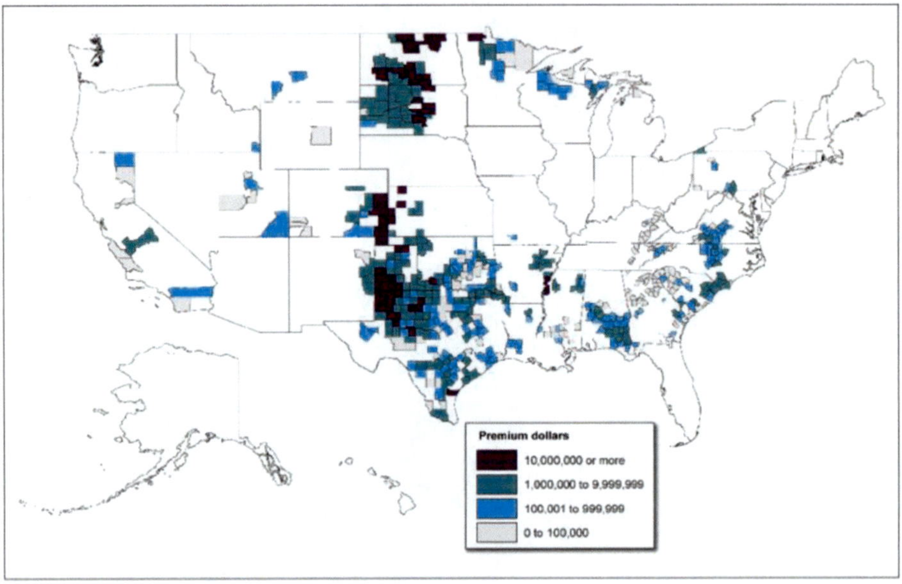

Source: GAO analysis of USDA's Risk Management Agency crop insurance data: MapInfo (map). | GAO-15-215.

Note: To identify areas with higher crop production risks, we determined the average of each county's 2013 county target premium rates for the five major crops—corn, soybeans, wheat, cotton, and grain sorghum. These averages were weighted by crop, crop type, and practice based on county premium dollars. The map shows the 20 percent of U.S. counties—510 counties—that had the highest average target premium rates.

Figure 2. Premiums for the Federal Crop Insurance Program in the Higher Risk Counties, 2013.

Figure 3 compares the estimated government crop insurance costs per dollar of expected crop value for the five major crops in the 510 higher risk counties with the costs in the 2,044 other U.S. counties from 2005 through 2013.[25] Total government crop insurance costs vary from year to year depending on weather-caused crop losses, crop prices, and farmers' decisions about how much insurance coverage to purchase.

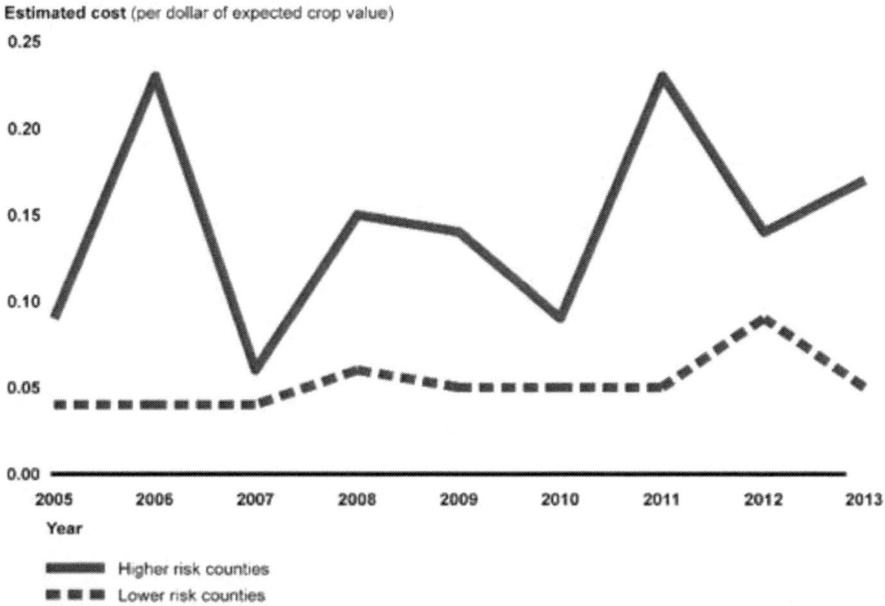

Source: GAO analysis of USDA's Risk Management Agency crop insurance data. | GAO-15-215.

Note: These estimated government costs are based on our analysis of Risk Management Agency data on loss claim payments to farmers, premium subsidies provided on behalf of farmers, premiums paid by farmers, administrative and operating expense subsidies paid to insurance companies, and underwriting gains paid to insurance companies. The crop data used for these estimates are corn, cotton, grain sorghum, soybeans, and wheat. Higher risk counties are those 510 U.S. counties with the highest average county target premium rates in 2013, and lower risk counties are the other 2,044 counties.

Figure 3. Estimated Federal Government Crop Insurance Costs per Dollar of Expected Crop Value for 2005 through 2013.

To control for variations in crop prices and farmers' purchase decisions, and to normalize the costs for higher risk counties and lower risk counties while still reflecting weather-caused crop losses, we expressed the estimated government costs in relation to expected crop value. As shown in figure 3, the costs in higher risk counties were substantially greater. Over the 9- year time frame, government costs averaged 14 cents per dollar of expected crop value in the higher risk counties and 5 cents per dollar in the other counties. For example, if two farms each had an expected crop value of $1 million, the higher risk farm would have had an average annual government cost of

$140,000, and the lower risk farm would have had an average annual government cost of $50,000. In 2013, the higher risk counties had a government cost of 17 cents per $1 of expected crop value, 3 cents higher than the average during the time frame, and the other counties had a government cost of 5 cents per $1 of expected crop value, the same as the time frame average.

Premium subsidies provided on behalf of farmers are a large component of government crop insurance costs. Figure 4 compares premium subsidies provided on behalf of farmers per dollar of expected crop value in the 510 higher risk counties with the premium subsidies in the 2,044 other counties from 1994 through 2013. Similar to the pattern shown in figure 3, figure 4 shows that premium subsidies in higher risk counties were substantially more than in the other counties. An important distinction between figure 3 and figure 4 is that figure 3 is indicative of differences in weather-related loss claim payments, which vary from year to year, while the measures of premium subsidies in figure 4 do not vary with weather-related loss claim payments and are related to the program design. In addition, figure 4 shows that the differences between higher risk counties and the other counties generally increased during the period from 1994 through 2013. Some of these increasing differences likely resulted from statutory increases in premium subsidy rates. For example, the Agricultural Risk Protection Act of 2000 increased premium subsidy rates. As a result, the premium subsidies provided on behalf of farmers increased from an average of 37 percent of the total premiums in 2000 to 60 percent in 2001, when the increased premium subsidy rates took effect. According to RMA officials, another likely reason for the increasing difference between higher risk counties and the other counties is that relatively more farmers in the higher risk counties changed from yield insurance to revenue insurance during the latter part of this time frame. Such a change causes farmers' premium rates and their premium subsidies to increase. However, the officials could not quantify the extent to which this change affected farmers' premium subsidies per dollar of expected crop value.

Farmers' net gains (i.e., loss claim payments received less premiums paid) from crop insurance offer another perspective on government costs in higher risk areas. Farmers' net gains are related to government costs. Premium subsidies are not only a large component of government costs but also an important factor in farmers' net gains from crop insurance. Figures 5 and 6 show, for 1994 through 2013, respectively, farmers' net gains per dollar of expected crop value and net gains per dollar of premium paid by farmers.

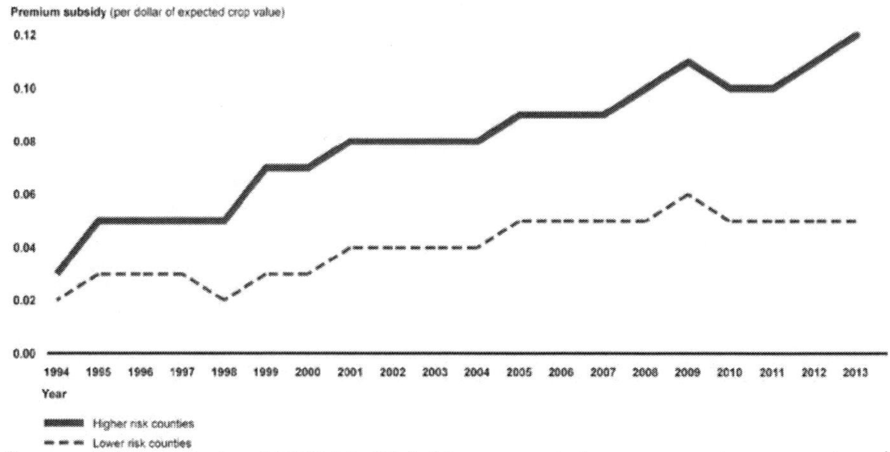

Source: GAO analysis of USDA's Risk Management Agency crop insurance data. | GAO-15-215.

Note: The five major crops used in these calculations are corn, cotton, grain sorghum, soybeans, and wheat. Higher risk counties are those 510 U.S. counties with the highest average county target premium rates in 2013, and lower risk counties are the other 2,044 counties.

Figure 4. Federal Crop Insurance Program Premium Subsidies Provided on Behalf of Farmers per Dollar of Expected Crop Value, 1994 through 2013.

If a farmer's net gain per dollar of premium paid is more than zero, it means the farmer received more in loss claim payments than he or she paid in premiums. As shown in these two figures, farmers' net gains fluctuated from year to year. Weather was a key factor for some of the years. For example, in the higher risk counties, farmers' net gains from crop insurance were relatively high in 2011 when areas of the Great Plains experienced a severe drought. Similarly, in the other areas, farmers' net gains were relatively high in 2012 when a large portion of the United States, including parts of the Corn Belt, had a major drought. During the 20-year time frame, farmers' net gains from crop insurance averaged 9 cents per $1 of expected crop value in the higher risk counties and 2 cents per $1 of expected crop value in the lower risk counties. In addition, farmers in higher risk counties averaged $1.97 in net gains per $1 of premiums paid compared with net gains averaging $0.87 per $1 of premiums paid for farmers in the lower risk counties over the 20-year time frame.

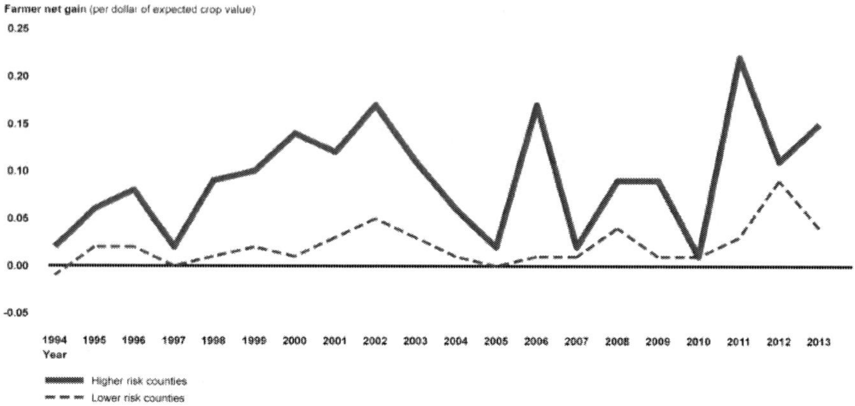

Source: GAO analysis of USDA's Risk Management Agency crop insurance data. | GAO-15-215.

Note: The five major crops used in these calculations are corn, cotton, grain sorghum, soybeans, and wheat. Higher risk counties are those 510 U.S. counties with the highest average county target premium rates in 2013, and lower risk counties are the other 2,044 counties.

Figure 5. Farmers' Net Gains from the Federal Crop Insurance Program per Dollar of Expected Crop Value, 1994 through 2013.

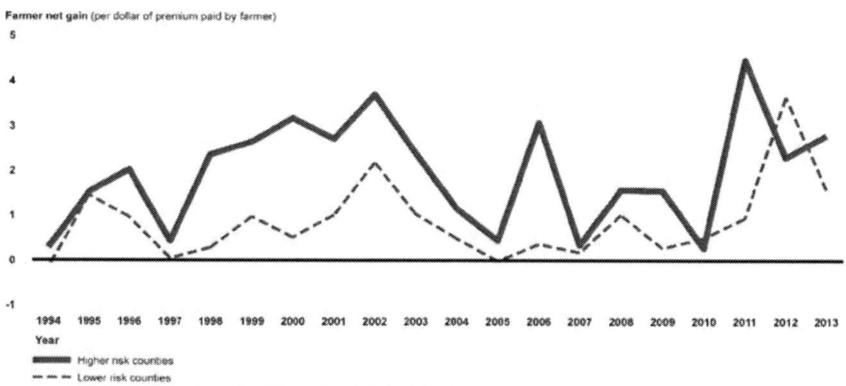

Source: GAO analysis of USDA's Risk Management Agency crop insurance data. | GAO-15-215.

Note: The five major crops used in these calculations are corn, cotton, grain sorghum, soybeans, and wheat. Higher risk counties are those 510 U.S. counties with the highest average county target premium rates in 2013, and lower risk counties are the other 2,044 counties.

Figure 6. Farmers' Net Gains from the Federal Crop Insurance Program per Dollar of Premiums Paid by Farmers, 1994 through 2013.

Figures 3, 4, 5, and 6 illustrate the extent to which higher risk areas have higher relative government costs, and farmers in those areas receive higher relative benefits. Furthermore, the difference between higher risk counties and lower risk counties in premium subsidies provided on behalf of farmers per dollar of expected crop value in 2013—11 cents per $1 versus 4 cents per $1, respectively, on average—indicates that the government's crop insurance costs might be reduced for farmers in higher risk counties without denying them sufficient risk protection. Specifically, if farmers in the other counties have sufficient risk protection while receiving premium subsidies of 4 cents per $1 of expected crop value, farmers in the higher risk counties might have sufficient risk protection with premium subsidies of less than 11 cents per $1 of expected crop value. Under the existing statutory premium subsidy structure, premium subsidies are a percentage of the premium, which means that the higher the premium, the higher the premium subsidies. As noted in a 2012 article in the *American Journal of Agricultural Economics*, riskier crops and regions have higher premium rates and thus receive more dollars in premium subsidies.[26] Analyses by agricultural economists also have addressed the premium subsidy structure. For example, a 2013 article suggested setting premium subsidies based on a given percentage of the crop value rather than as a percentage of the premiums.[27] According to our analysis, in 2013, if the premium subsidies in the higher risk counties had been 4 cents per $1 of expected crop value rather than 11 cents per $1, the government's cost would have been reduced by more than $600 million.

In addition to potential government cost savings, other factors relating to the premium subsidy structure include the following:

- Agricultural economists have questioned whether relatively higher premium subsidies going to higher risk areas affect farmers' crop production decisions (e.g., changes in quantity and allocation of acreage to individual crops). According to a 2012 article in the *American Journal of Agricultural Economics*,[28] the fact that significantly higher premium subsidies go to certain regions and crops suggests the potential for distortions of production decisions.
- Reductions in premium subsidies for higher risk areas could result in lower crop insurance participation and lower coverage levels among farmers in those areas. In the past, Congress has authorized ad hoc disaster assistance payments to help farmers whose crops were damaged or destroyed by natural disasters.[29] However, such programs

are costly and, given the nation's budgetary pressures, there is no guarantee that such programs would be available in the future.

- Several farm industry groups have opposed reductions in premium subsidies. For example, in March 2013, over 10 farm industry groups signed a letter that urged Congress to not make any changes in the crop insurance program that would discourage farmer participation.
- Crop production in higher risk areas may have disproportionately large environmental impacts. For example, a 2006 USDA study found that economically marginal land is, on average, more vulnerable to erosion, and generally has higher counts of imperiled species than other cropland.[30]

USDA's fiscal years 2014 to 2018 strategic plan includes an objective to maximize the return on taxpayer investment in USDA through enhanced stewardship activities of resources and focused program evaluations. Such evaluations could include an analysis of the government's crop insurance costs in higher risk areas. However, RMA does not monitor and report on the government's crop insurance costs in higher risk areas for the purpose of identifying potential cost savings through changes in program design, which would be consistent with USDA's objective. According to an RMA official, RMA does not monitor costs in higher risk areas to identify potential cost savings through changes in program design because RMA has not identified higher risk areas in the way that this report does. Without additional information from RMA on the government's crop insurance costs in higher risk areas, Congress may not have all the information it needs to make future assessments of the crop insurance program's design and costs.

RMA Premium Rate Changes in Areas with Higher Production Risks May Not Cover Expected Losses

RMA implemented changes to premium rates in 2014, decreasing some rates and increasing others, but our analysis of RMA data shows that, for some crops, RMA's higher risk premium rates may not cover expected losses.[31] RMA made changes to premium rates from 2013 to 2014, but its practice of phasing in changes to premium rates over time could have implications for actuarial soundness. Further, many premium rates in areas with higher production risks were lower than they should have been to cover expected losses and RMA's increases to these premium rates were not as high as they could have been under the law to fully cover expected losses.

RMA Made Changes to Premium Rates in Areas with Higher Crop Production Risks in 2014

We found that RMA adjusted higher risk county base premium rates and county target premium rates from 2013 to 2014 for the five major crops. The revisions in premium rates were in response to a 2010 study of its methodology and its periodic reviews of crop loss history.[32] The changes included increases and decreases of higher risk county base premium rates and county target premium rates for each of the five major crops. On average, RMA's various changes to premium rates from 2013 to 2014 resulted in decreases to county base premium rates and county target premium rates for corn and soybeans and increases for grain sorghum.[33] These changes also represented an increase in the percentage of county base premium rates that were aligned with county target premium rates for corn, soybeans, cotton, and grain sorghum, but not for wheat.

RMA has indicated in agency documents that it phases in new rates, especially those that require an increase, to keep premiums stable and provide farmers with predictable rates.[34] For example, in a 2013 document, the agency reported that it planned to slowly phase in changes to county base premium rates to mitigate the impact of a 2012 drought. However, phasing in changes to premium rates can have implications for improving actuarial soundness. For example, USDA's Office of Inspector General (OIG) reported in 2005 that, from crop years 2000 through 2003, when cotton crop losses were high relative to premiums, premium rates for cotton were decreased, unchanged, or increased only moderately[35] and, in these same 4 years, premiums were not sufficient to cover losses.[36] An RMA official told us that RMA uses judgment when changing county base premium rates, factoring in the agency's goal of maintaining stability for farmers in its decisions.

Many County Base Premium Rates Are Less than the County Target Premium Rates

When county base premium rates are lower than county target premium rates, RMA is required by statute to limit annual increases in premium rates to

20 percent of what the farmer paid for the same coverage in the previous year.[37] However, RMA uses discretion in deciding whether to raise rates by the full 20 percent or by a lesser amount (as indicated by its practice of phasing in rate changes).

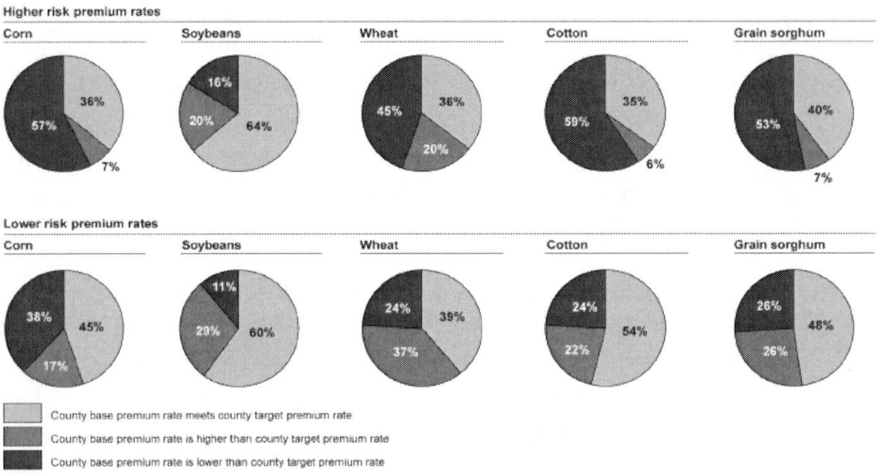

Source: GAO analysis of USDA's Risk Management Agency crop insurance data. | GAO-15-215.

Note: The percentages in this figure are based on an analysis of county target premium rates for each major practice (e.g., irrigated and nonirrigated) and major crop type (e.g., winter wheat or spring wheat) combination for each of the five major crops. A single county can have multiple county base premium and county target premium rates, depending on the number of combinations of crops, major practices, and crop types insured in the county. The term "higher risk premium rates" refers to the 2014 county target premium rates that were in the highest 20 percent of all county target premium rates for each crop, practice (e.g., irrigated and nonirrigated), and crop type (e.g., winter wheat and spring wheat). The term "lower risk premium rates" refers to the remaining 80 percent of county target premium rates. To calculate the percentages, we compared the county base premium rate with the county target premium rate for a single practice, and crop type combination and calculated the percentage difference. If the percentage difference between the county base premium rate and the county target premium rate was zero, we considered the county base premium rate as having met the county target premium rate. The percentages in the figure may not total 100 percent due to rounding.

Figure 7. The Percentage of County Base Premium Rates That Meet, Exceed, or Are Lower Than the County Target Premium Rates, 2014.

Based on our analysis, for the higher risk premium rates, half of county base premium rates for corn, cotton, and grain sorghum, and nearly half of county base premium rates for wheat are lower than the county target premium rates.[38] In contrast, for the lower risk premium rates, most of the county base premium rates for corn, cotton, grain sorghum, and wheat meet or exceed county target premium rates. Figure 7 shows the percentage of county base premium rates that meet, exceed, or are lower than county target premium rates in 2014.

We calculated percentage differences between county base premium rates and county target premium rates.[39] This provided a measure of the gap between the premium rate RMA charges a farmer (the county base premium rate) and the premium rate RMA should charge a farmer (the county target premium rate). For example, for nonirrigated cotton, one county had a county base premium rate of 26 percent and a county target premium rate of 32 percent. Thus, the county base premium rate was 6 percentage points less than the county target premium rate; however, the percentage difference was 23 percent.

For most higher risk premium rates where the county base premium rates were lower than the county target premium rates, the higher risk county base premium rates were within 20 percent of the county target premium rates in 2014, meaning RMA could fully align the rates in a single year. As shown in table 2, across the major crops, a larger percentage of county base premium rates are lower than county target premium rates by 20 percent or more for higher risk premium rates as compared to the lower risk premium rates.

Based on our analysis, from 2013 to 2014, RMA changed some county base premium rates by the full 20 percent allowed by the law. However, we also found that from 2013 to 2014, RMA did not raise county base premium rates as high as the law allows for many of the higher risk premium rates. For example, as shown in table 3, RMA made a lesser adjustment in about half of the county base premium rates for corn and cotton, and nearly half for grain sorghum that required a change of 20 percent or more to either meet or move closer to the county target premium rate. Table 3 shows the percentage of premium rates where a change of at least 20 percent was necessary to move the county base premium rate closer to the county target premium rate and where RMA did not use the full 20 percent authorized in statute.

Table 2. Percentage of County Base Premium Rates That Are Lower Than County Target Premium Rates by 20 Percent or More, 2014

Crop	Percentage Higher risk premium rates	Lower risk premium rates
Corn	31	14
Soybeans	2	1
Wheat	15	6
Cotton	20	6
Grain sorghum	24	6

Source: GAO analysis of USDA's Risk Management Agency crop insurance data. | GAO-15-215.

Note: The term "higher risk premium rates" refers to the 2014 county target premium rates that were in the highest 20 percent of all county target premium rates for each crop, practice (e.g., irrigated and nonirrigated), and crop type (e.g., winter wheat and spring wheat). The term "lower risk premium rates" refers to the remaining 80 percent of county target premium rates.

Table 3. Percentage of County Base Premium Rates Where the Risk Management Agency's Changes Were Less Than Needed to Meet the County Target Premium Rate, 2013 to 2014

	Increase to base rate when base rate was lower than the target rate		Decrease to base rate when base rate was higher than the target rate	
	Percentage		Percentage	
Crop	Higher risk premium rates	Lower risk premium rates	Higher risk premium rates	Lower risk premium rates
Corn	52	38	5	4
Soybeans	14	10	15	5
Wheat	38	22	18	14
Cotton	58	24	3	2
Grain sorghum	43	25	5	10

Source: GAO analysis of USDA's Risk Management Agency crop insurance data. | GAO-15-215.

Note: The percentages in this table are for those county base premium rates that required a change of at least 20 percent to either meet or move closer to the county target premium rate. The term "higher risk premium rates" refers to the 2014 county target premium rates that were in the highest 20 percent of all county target premium rates for each crop, practice (e.g., irrigated and nonirrigated), and crop type (e.g., winter wheat and spring wheat). The term "lower risk premium rates" refers to the remaining 80 percent of county target premium rates.

An RMA official told us that the agency strives for actuarial soundness not only nationwide, but also, at the county and crop level. Without sufficient increases to premium rates, where such increases are necessary, RMA's premium rates may not cover expected losses and may not be as high as they could be under the law, which may have implications for the actuarial soundness of the program. Among the higher risk premium rates, if the county base premium rates and the county target premium rates were identical, the federal government's total program costs in these areas would be lower because more premium dollars would be collected. For example, in analyzing data on premium dollars for 2013, our analysis showed that had the county base premium rates been aligned with the county target premium rates in higher risk counties, the federal government could have potentially collected tens of millions of dollars in additional premiums.[40]

However, the federal government's total program costs would not be reduced by the same amount as the additional premiums. The amount of the premium that the federal government provides on behalf of farmers (premium subsidy), about 62 percent, on average, would increase, but the portion of the premium that farmers pay would also increase. Thus, the additional premiums would reduce the government's costs. Also, when county base premium rates are lower than county target premium rates, farmers' production decisions may not be based on the true cost of their risk of loss due to weather-related events, such as drought; and, the federal government does not have information about the full amount of premium dollars the federal government should collect from farmers. Ensuring that the federal government has information about the full amount of premium dollars it should collect from farmers would be an activity consistent with RMA's core values.[41]

CONCLUSION

Federal crop insurance plays an important role in protecting farmers from losses from natural disasters and price declines, and the federal crop insurance program has become one of the most important programs in the farm safety net. RMA has overall responsibility for administering the program, including controlling costs. With increasing budgetary pressures, it is critical that federal resources are targeted as effectively as possible. One of USDA's strategic objectives is to maximize the return on taxpayer investment in the department through enhanced stewardship activities of resources and focused program evaluations. Such evaluations could include an analysis of the government's crop insurance costs in higher risk areas, where, as our analysis found, government costs are substantially higher than in other areas. However, RMA does not monitor and report on the government's crop insurance costs in higher risk areas to identify potential cost savings, which would be consistent with USDA's strategic objective. Without additional information from RMA on the government's crop insurance costs in higher risk areas, Congress may not have all the information it needs to make future assessments of the crop insurance program's design and costs.

In implementing premium rates, RMA seeks to balance its goals for participation and ensuring stability for farmers with maintaining an actuarially sound program. RMA updates its premium rates periodically, but there are continuing gaps between county base premium rates and county target premium rates. RMA has the ability to make changes to more quickly achieve greater actuarial soundness at the county and crop level but is not always doing so for areas with higher production risks. Without sufficient increases to premium rates, where applicable, RMA may not be taking all the actions available to achieve greater actuarial soundness. Additionally, moving to ensure that more county base premium rates meet county target premium rates will provide more information about the full costs to the federal government for insuring farmers in higher risk areas, consistent with the core value in RMA's fiscal years 2011 to 2015 strategic plan, and could also save federal funds.

RECOMMENDATIONS FOR EXECUTIVE ACTION

To better inform Congress in the future about crop insurance program costs, reduce present costs, and ensure greater actuarial soundness, we recommend that the Administrator of the U.S. Department of Agriculture's Risk Management Agency take the following two actions:

- Monitor and report on crop insurance costs in areas that have higher crop production risks.
- As appropriate, increase its adjustments of premium rates in areas with higher crop production risks by as much as the full 20 percent annually that is allowed by law.

AGENCY COMMENTS AND OUR EVALUATION

We provided USDA with a draft of this report for review and comment. We received written comments from the RMA Administrator. These comments are summarized below and reproduced in appendix III. In these comments, RMA disagreed with our first recommendation and agreed with our second recommendation. RMA stated that, consistent with the second recommendation, it will continue to revise premium rates in an appropriate, prudent, and actuarially sound manner, taking proper account of current rates and premium rate targets consistent with generally accepted actuarial practices.

In its written comments, RMA disagreed with our first recommendation to monitor and report on crop insurance costs in areas that have higher crop production risks and said it currently provides crop insurance data that have all the information necessary to determine crop insurance costs in all areas. RMA's website provides some information—such as county-level data on premiums, premium subsidies, loss claim payments, and loss ratios—that enables others to do some analysis of crop insurance costs. However, that information is not complete for the purpose of analyzing the government's costs and is not organized in a way that facilitates an understanding of the government's costs in higher risk areas. For example, regarding data on loss ratios (i.e., loss claim payments divided by premiums) that is on RMA's website, a recent article by an agricultural economist from the University of California notes that this loss ratio information for crop insurance (1) is not informative about and misrepresents the actuarial exposure borne by the [crop insurance] program and (2) by excluding administrative expenses, understates the extent of public expenditure on the program.[42] We agree with this assessment. Furthermore, placing data on a website does not constitute the monitoring of crop insurance costs. We continue to believe RMA can and should do more to monitor and report on crop insurance costs in higher risk areas, where we found government costs to be substantially higher than in other areas. As we said in this report, without additional information from RMA on the government's crop insurance costs in higher risk areas, Congress may not have all the information it needs to make future assessments of the crop insurance program's design and costs.

In addition, RMA commented on our analysis of the government's cost of the crop insurance program in higher risk areas. RMA said it has developed a definition of high-risk land, mapped out these areas, and applied significant premium surcharges. RMA said our definition of what we deem to be "higher risk areas" is much broader. RMA defines "high-risk land" as acreage with identifiable physical limitations, such as floodplains and high sand content soils. Our identification of higher risk areas (i.e., the 20 percent of counties that had the highest weighted average county target premium rates) enabled us to broadly assess crop insurance costs, and we believe this approach, which we discussed with RMA officials, was consistent with our purpose.

In its comment letter, RMA said our use of crop insurance costs (or benefits to farmers) per dollar of expected crop value "appears to exaggerate the difference in program costs in higher-risk areas versus other areas, or at least masks some important details." To present another perspective, RMA compared corn premium subsidies per acre for two states that had a large number of higher risk counties with two states that had no higher risk counties and stated that the premium subsidies per acre were similar amounts. We believe our use of a dollar-based measure (i.e., premium subsidies per dollar of expected crop value) is more appropriate than a physical measure (i.e., acres) for comparisons between costs and farmer benefits in higher risk areas and other areas. This is consistent with the methodology of a 2013 article by agricultural economists from The Ohio State University and the University of Illinois that compared net farm insurance payments using a dollar-based measure.[43]

Moreover, the use of a dollar-based measure is consistent with property insurance methods, which are based on the value of the property being insured. RMA stated that coverage levels were another offsetting effect, noting that growers in higher risk areas tend to choose lower coverage levels than in other areas, because higher premium rates make higher coverage less affordable. RMA appears to be suggesting that our analysis overlooks this difference, which is not true. As explained in our report, one of the reasons that we expressed estimated government costs in relation to expected crop value was to control for variations in farmers' purchase decisions. Farmers' decisions in selecting coverage levels vary between higher risk areas and other areas. According to our analysis, in 2013, farmers in higher risk counties chose to insure, on average, 67 percent of their expected crop value, while farmers in the other counties chose to insure, on average, 76 percent of their expected crop value. Thus, we used expected crop value—which is not affected by coverage levels—rather than insured crop value so that our analysis would not be distorted by differences in coverage levels.

RMA agreed with our second recommendation that, as appropriate, RMA increase its adjustments of premium rates in areas with higher crop production risks by as much as the full 20 percent annually that is allowed by law, saying it mirrors how premium rate adjustments are currently administered. However,

RMA stated it disagreed with our assessment of the extent to which premium rates need to be adjusted to the full amount allowed by statute and that adjusting premium rates fully to changes in premium rate targets would undercut the basic purpose of insurance—to provide financial stability. We continue to believe RMA's adjustment of premium rates should be consistent with insurance principles and the statutory directive to set premium rates that improve actuarial soundness. Furthermore, in its discussion of premium rates in "higher-risk" areas, RMA states that the report makes certain assumptions about premium rate targets in high risk areas that are not completely accurate and do not necessarily result in improved actuarial soundness. RMA further states that following each random variation to its fullest can subject growers to a roller-coaster ride of ups and downs in their premiums. RMA presented a simulation of yields and losses, showing that adjusting premium rates by less than needed to meet the premium rate target leads to a smaller variation in rates.

RMA's simulation suggested that the agency's current method of adjusting premium rates will yield an average premium rate that is actuarially sound at the national level. We agree that RMA's average premium rate, nationwide, may allow the program to be considered actuarially sound. However, our analysis focused on RMA's practices in charging premium rates in areas with higher production risks that may be lower or higher than the actuarially sound premium rate. In addition, RMA's simulation did not account for systematic variation in risk at the county and crop level. As we concluded, RMA could more quickly achieve actuarial soundness at the county and crop level. Moreover, as we stated, charging premium rates that are less than the actuarially sound premium rates could also have implications for total costs to the federal government in areas with higher production risks. Thus, we continue to believe that increasing the adjustments of premiums rates in areas with higher crop production risk by as much as the full 20 percent annually that is allowed by law is prudent and in keeping with sound fiscal practices.

Steve D. Morris
Director,
Natural Resources and Environment

Appendix I: Objectives, Scope, and Methodology

Our objectives were to determine, for areas with higher crop production risks, (1) the government's cost of the crop insurance program and (2) the extent to which RMA's premium rates, as implemented, cover expected losses.

To address these objectives, we reviewed relevant provisions of the Food, Conservation, and Energy Act of 2008 (2008 farm bill) and the Agricultural Act of 2014 (2014 farm bill); other statutes; and U.S. Department of Agriculture (USDA), regulations; and we analyzed crop insurance program data from RMA. We interviewed USDA officials, including officials from RMA, and reviewed documents they provided, such as, descriptions of the agency's methodology for calculating premium rates.

To address the first objective, we analyzed RMA crop insurance program data for the crop years 1994 through 2013; that is, those years for which complete data were available at the time we performed our work. We analyzed data for five major crops—corn, soybeans, wheat, cotton, and grain sorghum. These five crops represented 86 percent of the total crop insurance premiums for 2013. To identify areas with higher production risks, we used 2013 county target premium rates—that is, the rates that RMA calculates for each county (and crop, practice, and crop-type, combination) based on the county's loss history.[1] We calculated a weighted average county target premium rate for each county in 2013 combining the county target premium rates for all five crops, all of the crops' practices and crop types, using actual 2013 premium dollars as weights for these county weighted averages.[2, 3]

We used a weighted-average rather than a simple average because we wanted the average to reflect the relative importance of the different crop, practice, and crop-type combinations RMA used for premium calculations in 2013. Additionally, the use of a weighted-average county target premium rate allowed us to calculate a single measure for each county by which we could examine government costs in specific geographic areas.[4] We then ranked the counties from the highest to lowest weighted average target rate. We defined those counties ranked in the top 20 percent as "higher risk counties" and the remaining 80 percent of counties as "lower risk counties."[5] To calculate total government costs in these higher risk counties, we analyzed RMA data for 2005 through 2013.[6] We used the expected crop value to compare the costs in areas with higher production risks to the costs in other areas. Expected crop value is equal to the expected crop production multiplied by the expected (or elected) crop price. However, we did not have information on expected crop prices, so we calculated expected crop value by dividing the liability dollars by the coverage rate. Finally, to address the first objective we interviewed RMA officials, reviewed USDA's and other studies that examined the costs of the crop insurance program and the role of premium subsidies, and consulted documents from other stakeholders, including farm industry groups.

To address the second objective, we analyzed RMA data on production-based (or yield) premium rates for the five major crops (corn, cotton, grain sorghum, soybeans, and wheat) for crop years 2013 and 2014. Production-based premium rates are RMA's premium rates for production-based policies and are used to determine the premium rates for revenue policies.[7] RMA provided us with data, for each crop, practice, and crop-type combination, on the county base premium rate and the county target premium rate. We used the same 2013 data on county target premium rates to identify higher risk counties in our first objective. Using the 2013 premium rate data, we ranked the county target premium rates from highest to lowest and identified the highest 20 percent of county target premium rates for each crop, practice, and crop-type combination. For a given crop, a single county may have multiple county target premium rates, depending on the number of combinations of practices (e.g., irrigated and nonirrigated) and crop types (e.g., winter wheat and spring wheat) insured in the county. For example, for wheat, a county may have county target premium rates for two practice and crop-type combinations—nonirrigated winter wheat and nonirrigated spring wheat—in which one or both of the premium rates may fall in the highest 20 percent in 2014. For example, for wheat, County A in state B had county target premium rates for two practice and crop-type combinations—nonirrigated winter wheat and nonirrigated spring wheat— that were in the highest 20 percent in 2014. In total, there were 40 combinations or rankings of crops, practices, and crop types. Thus, if a county target premium rate fell into the top 20 percent in its ranking, that county target premium rate was placed in the "higher risk premium rate" category. The remaining 80 percent were placed in the "lower risk premium rate" category. We compared each county base premium rate with the applicable county target premium rate identified above. In each instance, we compared the county base premium rate with the county target premium rate for a single practice, and crop-type combination, and calculated the percentage difference. We calculated the percentage difference by subtracting the county base premium rate from the county target premium rate and dividing the result by the county base premium rate. If the percentage difference between the county base premium rate and the county target premium rate was zero, we considered the county base premium rate as having met the county target premium rate. If the percentage difference was greater than zero, we placed the county base premium rate in the "lower than" category; and, if the percentage difference was less than zero, we placed the county base rate in the "higher than" category. Table 4 provides details on the crop-type and practice combinations included in this review. Finally, we interviewed RMA officials in headquarters and two field offices regarding the agency's method for setting and implementing changes to county premium rates. We judgmentally selected the field offices based on the offices having had experience implementing premium rates in areas with higher production risks. We also reviewed studies that examined the agency's methodology for assigning premium rates and reviewed relevant audits by USDA's Office of the Inspector General.

Table 4. GAO's Grouping of the Risk Management Agency's Practice and Crop-Type Combinations

Practice and crop type	Practice code	Crop-type code
Corn (0041)		
Irrigated - grain	002	016
Nonirrigated - grain	003	016
Soybeans (0081)		
Irrigated - commodity	002	091
Irrigated - no specified type	002	997
Not following another crop (NFAC) irrigated - commodity	094	091
NFAC irrigated - no specified type	094	997
Following another crop (FAC) irrigated - commodity	095	091
FAC irrigated - no specified type	095	997
Nonirrigated - commodity	003	091
Nonirrigated - no specified type	003	997
NFAC nonirrigated - commodity	053	091
NFAC nonirrigated - no specified type	053	997
FAC nonirrigated - commodity	043	091
FAC nonirrigated - no specified type	043	997
Wheat (0011)		
Irrigated - winter	002	011
Irrigated - spring	002	012
Irrigated - no specified type	002	997
Irrigated - durum	002	015
Nonirrigated - winter	003	011
Nonirrigated - spring	003	012
Nonirrigated - no specified type	003	997

Practice and crop type	Practice code	Crop-type code
Nonirrigated - durum	003	015
Continuous cropping - winter	004	011
Continuous cropping - spring	004	012
Continuous cropping - no specified type	004	997
Continuous cropping - durum	004	015
Summerfallow - winter	005	011
Summerfallow - spring	005	012
Summerfallow - no specified type	005	997
Summerfallow - durum	005	015
Waterfallow - spring	006	012
Cotton (0021)		
Irrigated - no specified type	002	997
Nonirrigated - no specified type	003	997
NFAC nonirrigated - no specified type	053	997
FAC nonirrigated - no specified type	043	997
Nonirrigated skip row - no specified type	063	997
Grain sorghum (0051)		
Irrigated - no specified type	002	997
FAC irrigated- no specified type	095	997
NFAC irrigated - no specified type	094	997
Nonirrigated - no specified type	003	997

Source: GAO analysis of USDA's Risk Management Agency crop insurance data. | GAO-15-215.

Note: According to Risk Management Agency documents, the practice, NFAC, refers to not following another crop and the practice, FAC, refers to following another crop.

For the various data used in our analyses, as discussed, we generally reviewed related documentation, interviewed knowledgeable officials, and reviewed related internal controls information to evaluate the reliability of these data. In each case, we concluded that the data were sufficiently reliable for the purposes of this report.

We conducted this performance audit from December 2013 to February 2015 in accordance with generally accepted government auditing standards. Those standards require that we plan and perform the audit to obtain sufficient, appropriate evidence to provide a reasonable basis for our findings and conclusions based on our audit objectives. We believe that the evidence obtained provides a reasonable basis for our findings and conclusions based on our objectives.

APPENDIX II: PREMIUMS IN THE 10 PERCENT OF COUNTIES WITH THE HIGHEST PREMIUM RATES, 2013

Figure 8 shows the 255 counties that were the riskiest 10 percent of counties in terms of average county target premium rates. These counties are shaded on the basis of their 2013 premium dollars to show which risky counties had the most crop insurance.

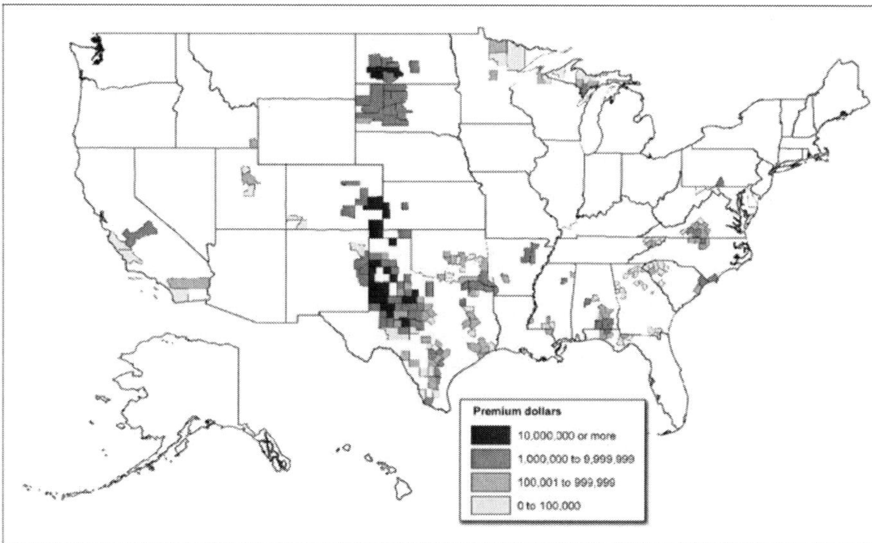

Source: GAO analysis of USDA's Risk Management Agency crop insurance data: MapInfo (map). | GAO-15-215.

Note: To identify areas with higher crop production risks, we determined the average of each county's 2013 county target premium rates for the five major crops—corn, soybeans, wheat, cotton, and grain sorghum. These averages were weighted by crop, crop type, and practice based on county premium dollars. The map shows the 10 percent of U.S. counties—255 counties—that had the highest average target premium rates.

Figure 8. Premiums in the Higher Risk Counties, 2013.

APPENDIX III: COMMENTS FROM THE U.S. DEPARTMENT OF AGRICULTURE

USDA

United States Department of Agriculture

Farm and Foreign Agricultural Services
Risk Management Agency

JAN 0 6 2014

TO: Steve D. Morris
Director, Natural Resources and Environment
U.S. Government Accountability Office

FROM: Brandon Willis
Administrator
Risk Management Agency

SUBJECT: U.S. Department of Agriculture Comments- U.S. Government Accountability Office Draft Report, Crop Insurance: In Areas with Higher Crop Production Risks, Costs Are Higher and Premiums May Not Cover Expected Losses, GAO-15-215 (361542)

This GAO audit report contains two separate parts, and associated recommendations. The first recommendation is to "[m]onitor and report on crop insurance costs in areas that have higher crop production risks." RMA does not agree with this recommendation as RMA currently provides crop insurance data that has all the information necessary to determine crop insurance costs in all areas. This information can be broken out by crop and by state. RMA does not believe that providing an additional report is a wise use of resources when this information is already available and there is no commonly accepted definition of high risk areas.

The second recommendation is "[a]s appropriate, increase its adjustments of premium rates in areas with higher crop production risks by as much as the full 20 percent annually that is allowed by law."

RMA agrees with the recommendation since it mirrors how premium rate adjustments are currently administered, but based upon the report likely disagrees regarding the extent that rates need to be adjusted to the full amount allowed by statute. Following each random variation of a premium rate's target to its fullest can subject growers to a rollercoaster ride of ups and downs in their premium rates, without actually improving long-term actuarial soundness. It also undercuts the basic purpose of insurance – to provide financial stability.

RMA

Deputy Administrator for Compliance
1400 Independence Ave., SW • STOP 0806 • Washington, DC 20250-0806

The Risk Management Agency Administers and Oversees
All Programs Authorized Under the Federal Crop Insurance Corporation

USDA is an Equal Opportunity Provider and Employer

Steve Morris
GAO 361542
Page 2

Part 1: Crop Insurance Costs in Higher-Risk Areas

This part of the audit report GAO defines high risk areas and estimates the crop insurance program costs in these areas, advocating a policy position of reducing premium subsidies. RMA has also developed a definition of high risk land, mapped out these areas (i.e. a flood plain), and applied significant premium rate surcharges. The audit report contains a different, and much broader definition of what it deems "higher-risk areas" than RMA's definition, which was provided to GAO.

The cost of the crop insurance program to taxpayers, or conversely, the benefit of the program to growers is measured as per dollar of expected crop value. This measure appears to exaggerate the difference in program costs in higher-risk areas versus other areas, or at least masks some important details.

For example, the report outlines that growers in high risk areas received 11 cents of premium subsidy per dollar of crop value in 2013, versus 4 cents of premium subsidy per dollar of crop value for other areas. This suggests that growers in high risk areas are receiving nearly three times the benefits versus other growers.

Table 1 presents another perspective. The table shows the 2014 average coverage level, subsidy per acre, and crop value per acre for a couple of states that account for a large share of the counties designated as "higher-risk" in the audit report (Texas and Oklahoma) and for a couple of states that contain no counties designated as "higher-risk" (Illinois and Indiana). Several important points emerge from this table.

Table 1: Average Coverage Level, Subsidy Per Acre, and Crop Value Per Acre

STATE	DATA	CORN	COTTON	SORGHUM	SOYBEANS	WHEAT	TOTAL
ILLINOIS	Avg Coverage Level	82%		70%	80%	72%	81%
	Avg. Subs. Per Acre	$23.43		$28.31	$13.65	$24.46	$19.24
	Avg Value Per Acre	$811.34		$393.06	$575.32	$409.51	$699.21
INDIANA	Avg Coverage Level	81%		70%	81%	74%	81%
	Avg. Subs. Per Acre	$25.89		$22.02	$17.26	$21.89	$21.73
	Avg Value Per Acre	$777.15		$328.61	$587.07	$449.29	$679.98
OKLAHOMA	Avg Coverage Level	69%	71%	68%	67%	70%	69%
	Avg. Subs. Per Acre	$28.45	$55.74	$26.36	$28.90	$20.40	$23.02
	Avg Value Per Acre	$664.07	$585.00	$183.33	$252.54	$210.64	$250.73
TEXAS	Avg Coverage Level	66%	67%	67%	67%	65%	66%
	Avg. Subs. Per Acre	$26.03	$54.71	$23.80	$32.88	$24.60	$37.34
	Avg Value Per Acre	$622.64	$512.45	$241.68	$281.57	$181.61	$389.03
TOTAL	Avg Coverage Level	80%	67%	67%	80%	68%	77%
	Avg. Subs. Per Acre	$24.47	$54.74	$24.17	$15.37	$22.70	$25.59
	Avg Value Per Acre	$777.91	$514.78	$234.99	$569.47	$212.00	$554.35

Steve Morris
GAO 361542
Page 3

First, the amount of subsidy per acre in higher-risk states is not that different from lower-risk states for corn, wheat, and sorghum. For example, the subsidy per acre for corn is $26.03 in Texas and $28.45 in Oklahoma, versus $25.89 in Indiana and $23.43 in Illinois. If a 200-acre corn farm in Texas versus a 200-acre corn farm in Indiana is compared, the subsidy benefit is approximately the same. This is because there are offsetting effects – in high risk areas there is less crop value per acre to be insured, which reduces the premium subsidy. In contrast, the average crop value per acre tends to be higher in low-risk areas, which increases the premium subsidy.

Another offsetting effect is coverage level. Growers in higher-risk areas tend to choose lower coverage levels because higher premium rates make higher coverage levels less affordable. For example, Texas has an average coverage level for corn of 66 percent as compared to 83 percent for Illinois.

One crop that stands out is cotton, with an average subsidy per acre that is well above the other crops. Cotton, more than any other crop, contributes to Texas being considered a high-risk area in the report, and accounts for much of the higher premium subsidy cost per acre. Texas accounts for a large share of cotton production in the U.S. This means that the report's proposal to reduce premium subsidy rates in high-risk areas will tend to affect cotton more than any other crop, and also affect Texas more than most other states.

The report recommends that RMA "monitor and report on crop insurance costs in areas that have higher production risks." However, RMA currently provides the relevant crop insurance data to determine crop insurance costs in all areas on its website.

Part 2: Premium Rates in "Higher-Risk" Areas

The second part of the report makes certain assumptions about premium rate targets in high risk areas that are not completely accurate and do not necessarily result in improved actuarial soundness. The report first identifies instances where RMA increased premium rates by less than the 20 percent limit allowed by law. The report then suggests that premium rates should have been increased by the full 20 percent.

A premium rate target represents a current snapshot of risk based on accumulated loss data. The challenge with premium rate targets is that they are always moving up or down with each update of loss experience, following a random path based on the weather events that occurred since the previous update. In other words, targets are a 'noisy' signal. Following each random variation of a premium rate's target to its fullest, as GAO recommends, can subject growers to a rollercoaster ride of ups and downs in their premium rates, without actually improving long-term actuarial soundness. It also undercuts the basic purpose of insurance – to provide financial stability.

To illustrate this point, a simulation of yields and losses over a 10,000 year period was undertaken. Throughout the simulation, the premium rate targets were updated every few years, like what is currently done for the Federal crop insurance program. The premium rate charged to the producer in this simulation was adjusted in two ways; full adjustment to target ('GAO Suggested Method') and a

Steve Morris
GAO 361542
Page 4

moderated adjustment to target ('RMA Method') similar to what is done today for the crop insurance program. The results are shown in the graphs and table below, with the GAO Suggested Method on the left and the RMA Method on the right.

The graphs show the annual premium rate changes across the 'years' of the simulation. As expected, the GAO Suggested Method results in greater rate changes (often reaching the 20 percent maximum) than the RMA Method. However, the long-run actuarial performance of the two methods is the same.

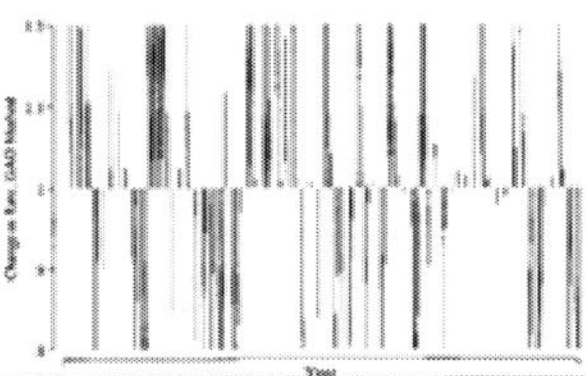

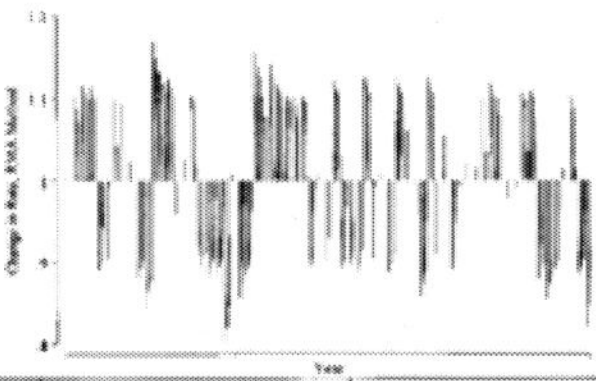

	GAO Method	RMA Method	Percent Difference
Variance of Rate Changes	0.0148	0.0081	-45%
Long-Run Average Rate	4.07%	4.07%	0%

The table shows that the long-run average rate for both methods is 4.07 percent – an actuarially sound rate given the parameters of the simulation. However, the RMA Method results in 45 percent less variation rates than the GAO Suggested Method. The simulation demonstrates that movements toward targets can be moderated without compromising long-run actuarial soundness. A rate does not have to go all the way to its target in a single year to be an actuarially sound rate.

This point is also supported by the 2014 premium rates for the counties designated in the report as "higher-risk"[1]. Table 2 divides the higher-risk counties into those that had a rate increase, decrease, or no change from 2013 to 2014. The table then compares the average change in rates published by RMA versus what the rate would have been if the GAO suggested approach had been followed.

The analysis presented here is based on RMA's best estimate of what GAO considered to be higher-risk based on the description of their methodology provided in the report.

Steve Morris
GAO 361542
Page 5

Table 2: Comparison of RMA Published Rates Versus GAO Suggested Rates in "Higher-Risk" Counties, 2014

	RMA Published Rates		GAO Rates*	
	Average Change from 2013	Average Premium Rate	Average Change from 2013	Average Premium Rate
Counties with a Rate Increase	11.0%	25.1%	13.2%	25.8%
Counties with a Rate Decrease	-12.1%	23.9%	-13.6%	23.2%
Counties with No Change in Rate	0.0%	26.8%	0.0%	23.4%
Average for All Counties		**24.7%**		**24.7%**

* GAO Rates: Premium rates based on GAO's recommendation to move rates all the way to their targets, subject to the 20 percent limit for rate increases specified in the Federal Crop Insurance Act.

In 2014, the average premium rate increase was 11.0 percent and the decrease was 12.1 percent. Overall, the resulting average premium rate in the higher-risk counties was 24.7 percent. Similar to what occurred in the simulation, if the GAO suggested approach had been used to determine premium rates, there would have been somewhat larger changes overall – an average increase of 13.2 percent and an average decrease of 13.6 percent. Also similar to the simulation, the GAO suggested approach would have produced the same simple average premium rate for higher-risk counties as the premium rates actually published by RMA – 24.7 percent. The GAO suggested approach produces a larger variability in rates, but results in a similar average rate.

Premium rates will tend to be farthest away from their targets in the year when the targets are revised. Over time, as premium rates adjust, this difference narrows – until the targets are revised again and the process starts over.

Generally, RMA revises premium rate targets for the major crops every 3 years to incorporate newly-accumulated loss data. However, for the crops analyzed in this audit report, RMA did not wait the full three years and revised the premium rate targets ahead of schedule in both 2013 and in 2014. This was done, in part, because of the recent significant loss events that had occurred in the Southern Plains and in the Corn Belt. The recent updates, combined with the loss events, contributed to the report's observation of a disproportionate number of counties below target.

Steve Morris
GAO 361542
Page 6

RMA's early updating of premium rate targets also resulted in larger premium rates increases than would have otherwise been the case, especially in those areas where significant losses occurred. If RMA had elected not to update targets early, premium rates would have been generally closer to their unchanged targets. This would have made the premium rates less subject to the report's criticism, but they would not have been as responsive to losses.

Although premium rate changes are moderated, they still make rapid progress toward their targets. In 2014, a year in which targets were updated, 46 percent of the rates in the higher risk counties moved to their targets that same year. For 2015, 73 percent of rates are at their targets. By 2016, it is expected that around 87 percent will be at their targets. Of those remaining rates that are unlikely to meet their targets in 2016, a significant portion are due to the limit required by the Act that no premium rate may increase by more than 20 percent, and not due to the moderation of annual changes by RMA.

The report makes a recommendation for RMA to, "...as appropriate, increase its adjustments of premium rates in areas with higher crop production risks by as much as the full 20 percent annually that is allowed by law." The recommendation is based on the assumption that faster movement to targets necessarily results in improved actuarial soundness – an assumption that is not completely accurate. Consistent with the recommendation, RMA will continue to revise premium rates in an appropriate, prudent and actuarially sound manner, taking proper account of current rates and premium rate targets consistent with generally accepted actuarial practices.

End Notes

[1] This estimate includes projected costs associated with new crop insurance provisions in the Agricultural Act of 2014.

[2] GAO, Fiscal Exposures: Improving Cost Recognition in the Federal Budget, GAO-14-28 (Washington, D.C.: Oct. 29, 2013).

[3] GAO, Crop Insurance: Savings Would Result from Program Changes and Greater Use of Data Mining, GAO-12-256 (Washington, D.C.: Mar. 13, 2012) and 2013 Annual Report: Actions Needed to Reduce Fragmentation, Overlap, and Duplication and Achieve Other Financial Benefits, GAO-13-279SP (Washington, D.C.: Apr. 9, 2013).

[4] GAO, Crop Insurance: Considerations in Reducing Federal Premium Subsidies, GAO-14-700 (Washington, D.C.: Aug. 8, 2014).

[5] Federal Crop Insurance Act § 508(i)(1) (codified at 7 U.S.C. § 1508(i)(1)). Specifically, the law directs RMA to adopt, as soon as practicable, rates and coverages that will improve the actuarial soundness of RMA's insurance operations for those crops that are determined to be insured at rates that are not actuarially sound, except that no rate may be increased by an amount of more than 20 percent over the comparable rate of the preceding crop year. 7 U.S.C. § 1508(i)(1). According to RMA, it must set premium rates and implement rate changes in a timely manner to cover expected losses and a reasonable reserve.

[6] The Actuarial Standards Board (ASB), which is the standards-setting entity of the U.S. actuarial profession, has noted that the phrase "actuarial soundness" has different meanings in different contexts, and that its meaning in a particular context might be imposed by an entity outside of the actuarial profession (e.g., a statute). The ASB's standards state that if an actuary defines a process or result as "actuarially sound," the actuary should define the meaning of "actuarially sound" in that context. As stated previously, current law directs RMA to set premium rates and coverage levels that improve actuarial soundness of the federal crop insurance program.

[7] Federal Crop Insurance Act § 508(i)(2) (codified at 7 U.S.C. § 1508(i)(2)).

[8] RMA documents indicate that the agency also implemented additional recommendations from the 2010 study such as an adjustment of pre-1995 loss data and the use of weather data experience when adjusting premium rates.

[9] This request was originally made by Senator Tom Coburn, former Ranking Member, Committee on Homeland Security and Governmental Affairs.

[10] The five major crops represented 86 percent of the total crop insurance premiums for 2013.

[11] An RMA official knowledgeable about the agency's process for setting county target premium rates told us that these premium rates reflect the best estimates that RMA has regarding the risk associated with insuring a crop in a county.

[12] We calculated alternative cutoffs, including 50th, 70th, 90th and 95th percentiles. We determined that the 80th percentile cutoff is a compromise between having the cutoff too high—such as the 95th percentile, which might have too few higher risk counties to allow for meaningful estimates—and, having too broad of a cutoff—the 50th percentile cutoff, for example.

[13] According to RMA, total government costs are equal to loss claim payments to farmers minus premiums and other income received by the government plus premium subsidies provided on behalf of farmers plus administrative and operating expenses paid to insurance companies plus other costs (e.g., RMA's salaries and expenses for administering the program).

[14] We used the same 2013 production-based (or yield) county target premium rates data from RMA to identify areas with higher production risks in both objectives. Productionbased premium rates are RMA's published county premium rates for production-based policies and are used to determine the premium rates for revenue policies, which protect against crop revenue loss resulting from declines in production, price, or both. Most crop insurance policies are either production-based or revenue policies. For production-based policies, a

farmer can receive a payment if there is a production loss relative to the farmer's historical production per acre.

[15] Federal Crop Insurance Act § 502 (codified at 7 U.S.C. § 1502). According to RMA, Congress first authorized federal crop insurance in the 1930s along with other initiatives to help agriculture recover from the combined effects of the Great Depression and the Dust Bowl.

[16] For the purposes of this report, as appropriate, we report data in calendar, fiscal, or crop years. According to ERS, a crop year (also known as a marketing year) is the 12-month period starting with the month when the harvest of a specific crop typically begins. For example, the 2008 wheat crop year was June 1, 2008, through May 30, 2009.

[17] RMA calculates a farmer's premium rate using a formula that includes the farmer's actual production history yield (the expected yield), a reference yield (the average yield for all farmers planting a particular crop in a county), the county base premium rate, the crop type and practice, geographic dispersion of the land insured, and a coverage differential (fractions assigned to the various coverage levels).

[18] RMA is required by statute to limit yearly increases in premium rates to 20 percent of what the farmer paid for the same coverage in the previous year. RMA uses a capping procedure so that changes to any component of the premium rate do not increase the rate by more than the 20 percent limit set by statute.

[19] RMA reports that, generally, it conducts reviews of premium rates for any given crop every 3 years.

[20] In addition, premium subsidy rates can vary based on the geographic diversity of the land parcels being insured. For example, at the 70 percent coverage level, the premium subsidy rate is 80 percent for an enterprise unit and 59 percent for a basic unit. An enterprise unit consists of all insurable acreage of the same insured crop in the county in which the farmer has a share on the date coverage begins for the crop year. In contrast, a basic unit consists only of acreage with the same farmer and landowner.

[21] Farmers select a coverage level—that is, the percentage of their normal yield or revenue they want to insure. In 2012, more than half of the enrolled corn and soybean acres were at coverage levels above 70 percent.

[22] R. Dismukes and J. Glauber, "Why Hasn't Crop Insurance Eliminated Disaster Assistance?", Amber Waves, USDA Economic Research Service (June 2005).

[23] These averages of 2013 target premium rates were weighted by county premium dollars. Specifically, we calculated weighted-average county target premium rates for each county based on the 2013 county premium dollars associated with each practice-crop type combination. We used these weighted-average county target premium rates because this measure indicates crop production risks, while being related to government costs through the weighting of the rates by county premium dollars. We used a weighted-average rather than a simple average because we wanted the average to reflect the relative importance of the different crop, practice, and crop-type combinations RMA used for premium calculations in 2013. Moreover, the use of weighted-average county target premium rates provides a single measure that facilitates the examination of government costs by geographic area. We selected 2013 because it was the most recent year for which complete RMA data on program costs was available at the time we did this analysis. The five major crops represented 86 percent of the total crop insurance premiums for 2013.

[24] Our use of the 20 percent of counties that had the highest average county target premium rates is for illustration purposes. In this report, we generally use these 20 percent of counties to examine crop insurance costs in areas that have higher crop production risks. We recognize that alternative groupings (or cutoff values) could be used. For example, a map showing the

10 percent of counties that had the highest average county target premium rates and the premiums in those counties is in appendix II.

[25] Expected crop value is equal to the expected crop production multiplied by the expected (or elected) crop price. However, we did not have information on expected crop prices, so we calculated expected crop value by dividing the liability dollars by the coverage rate.

[26] Keith H. Coble and Barry J. Barnett, "Why Do We Subsidize Crop Insurance?" American Journal of Agricultural Economics (November 2012).

[27] Carl Zulauf and Gary Schnitkey, "Distribution of Crop Insurance Net Farm Payments by Crop and State," in farmdoc daily, (Department of Agricultural and Consumer Economics, University of Illinois at Urbana-Champaign, February 2013), accessed October 28, 2013, http://farmdocdaily.illinois.edu/2013/02/distribution-of-crop-insurance.html.

[28] Barry Goodwin and Vincent Smith, "What Harm is Done by Subsidizing Crop Insurance?" American Journal of Agricultural Economics (December 2012).

[29] In some instances, farmers had to have crop insurance to be eligible for the ad hoc disaster assistance and, in other instances, this was not required.

[30] USDA Economic Research Service, Environmental Effects of Agricultural Land-Use Change: The Role of Economics and Policy, Economic Research Report Number 25 (August 2006).

[31] In this section, the term "higher risk premium rates" refers to areas with higher production risks. Specifically, we examined county base premium rates and county target premium rates for 2013 and 2014. The county target premium rates are in the highest 20 percent of all county target premium rates for each crop, practice (e.g., irrigated and nonirrigated), and crop type (e.g., winter wheat and spring wheat). For a given crop, a single county can have multiple county target premium rates depending on the number of different practices and crop types insured in the county. We analyzed each practice-crop type combination separately. The total number of county target premium rates in the highest 20 percent, by crop, are: corn (708), soybeans (722), wheat (750), cotton (233), and grain sorghum (226). The practice-crop type combinations are shown in the appendix I table.

[32] RMA reported that it made partial revisions to county base premium rates and county target premium rates for corn and soybeans in 2012 in response to a study of its methodology.

[33] On average, RMA's various changes from 2013 to 2014 also resulted in decreases to irrigated wheat and cotton and increases to nonirrigated wheat. For nonirrigated cotton, RMA increased county base premium rates and decreased county target premium rates.

[34] As far back as 1995, RMA expressed concern about raising premium rates citing the possibility that abrupt increases may discourage participation in the federal crop insurance program by farmers.

[35] U.S. Department of Agriculture Office of the Inspector General, Cotton Crop Insurance Premium Rates, No. 05601-7-At (Washington, D.C: Feb. 10, 2005).

[36] In response to the OIG's 2005 report, RMA said that the agency's reason for delaying the increase in premium rates for cotton was, in part, to maintain stability in the premium rates for farmers.

[37] When county base premium rates are higher than county target premium rates, RMA can exceed 20 percent in adjusting the county base premium rate to reach the county target premium rate.

[38] County base premium rates in higher risk counties for soybeans largely meet the county target premium rates.

[39] We calculated the percentage difference by subtracting the county base premium rate from the county target premium rate and dividing the result by the county base premium rate. The calculated percentages would be somewhat different if we divided by the county target

premium rate instead. By dividing by the county base premium rate, the percentage differences indicate the percentage change in the county base premium rate that would be necessary for it to reach the county target premium rate.

[40] Several factors are important to consider regarding our estimate of additional premiums. First, we only reviewed yield premium rates, and the estimated additional premium refers only to those types of premium rates. Second, our estimate does not adjust for the fact that RMA's annual premium rate changes are constrained by the statutory 20 percent limit on such changes. Finally, however, it also does not adjust for the potential effect of base rates being less than target rates on farmers' crop production decisions (e.g., changes in quantity and allocation of acreage to individual crops and changes in coverage levels).

[41] RMA's fiscal years 2011 to 2015 strategic plan includes the goal of "making the Agency's management processes more open so that the public can learn how RMA supports Americans every day and in every way."

[42] Brian Davern Wright, "Multiple Peril Crop Insurance." Choices (3rd Quarter 2014).

[43] Zulauf and Schnitkey, "Distribution of Crop Insurance Net Farm Payments by Crop and State."

End Notes for Appendix I

[1] An RMA official knowledgeable about the agency's process for setting county target premium rates told us that these premium rates reflect the best estimates that RMA has regarding the risk associated with insuring a crop in a county.

[2] We selected 2013 because it was the most recent year for which complete RMA data on program costs was available at the time we performed this analysis.

[3] We recognize that an area or location may be high risk for one crop or crop type or practice type but not for a different crop. However, by using 2013 premium dollars to weight the average of the different target rates used in a given county, we maintain that such a calculation allows a reasonable average approximation of a location's production risk.

[4] We selected 2013 because it was the most recent year for which complete RMA data on program costs was available at the time we performed this analysis.

[5] We calculated alternative cutoffs for our high versus low risk definition, including 50th, 70th, 90th and 95th percentiles. The 80th percentile cutoff is a compromise between having the cutoff too high, such as the 95th percentile, which might have too few high risk counties to allow meaningful estimates of the high risk counties' characteristics; and say, a 50th percentile cutoff, which might be too broad a definition of "higher risk".

[6] According to RMA, total government costs are equal to loss claim payments to farmers minus premiums and other income received by the government plus premium subsidies provided on behalf of farmers plus administrative and operating expenses paid to insurance companies plus other costs (for example, as RMA's salaries and expenses for administering the program).

[7] Most crop insurance policies are either production-based or revenue policies. For production-based policies, a farmer can receive a payment if there is a production loss relative to the farmer's historical production per acre. Revenue policies protect against crop revenue loss resulting from declines in production, price, or both.

INDEX

A

accounting, 8
adjustment, 39, 53, 59, 71
agricultural producers, 38
agriculture, 2, 3, 20, 27, 28, 38, 72
alfalfa, 7, 27
apples, 3
appropriations, 20
assessment, 57, 59
assets, 20
audit(s), 38, 62, 63
average revenue, 11

B

bankruptcy, 27
banks, 3
base, 39, 40, 41, 51, 52, 53, 54, 55, 56, 61, 72, 73, 74
base rate(s), 54, 62, 74
benefits, 23, 29, 49, 58
biomass, 27
budget resolution, 29

C

cash, 28
catfish, 27
cattle, 11
Census, 16
challenges, 36
color, 43, 44
combined effect, 72
commercial, 27
commodity, vii, 1, 2, 3, 6, 7, 9, 10, 11, 15, 17, 27, 28, 62
communities, 38
compensation, 28
compliance, 27
Congress, vii, 1, 2, 3, 4, 29, 36, 41, 49, 50, 56, 57, 72
Congressional Budget Office, 28, 33, 36
conservation, 27
consolidation, 30
contamination, 27
controversial, 28
cost, vii, 2, 3, 4, 11, 21, 28, 34, 36, 37, 42, 45, 49, 50, 55, 56, 57, 60
cost saving, 49, 50, 56
cotton, 2, 4, 11, 14, 16, 18, 19, 27, 37, 39, 43, 44, 45, 47, 48, 51, 53, 60, 61, 64, 73
covering, 36
crop producers, 6
crop production, 34, 36, 37, 38, 42, 43, 44, 49, 56, 57, 58, 59, 60, 64, 72, 73, 74
crops, vii, 1, 2, 3, 4, 5, 6, 7, 8, 10, 11, 13, 14, 16, 18, 19, 25, 27, 28, 29, 30, 34, 35, 37, 39, 43, 44, 47, 48, 49, 50, 51, 52, 53, 60, 61, 64, 71, 72, 74

D

deficit, 2, 28, 29
Department of Agriculture, 33
disaster, 3, 4, 7, 28, 41, 49, 73
disaster assistance, 7, 28, 41, 49, 73
dispersion, 39, 72
distortions, 49
distribution, 16, 18, 73
diversity, 15, 72
draft, 57
drought, 3, 11, 16, 26, 30, 34, 36, 39, 41, 42, 44, 47, 51, 55

E

Economic Research Service (ERS), 18, 36, 72, 73
election, 10
environmental impact, 50
erosion, 50
ERS, 36, 72
evidence, 38, 63
expenditures, 17, 18, 25
exposure, 26, 57

F

Farm Bill, 27, 29, 31
farm size, 17
farmers, 2, 3, 7, 9, 11, 18, 23, 26, 28, 29, 30, 33, 35, 36, 37, 39, 40, 41, 42, 44, 45, 46, 47, 49, 51, 55, 56, 58, 71, 72, 73, 74
farms, 4, 14, 15, 17, 18, 45
federal crop insurance program, vii, 1, 2, 3, 4, 8, 20, 23, 27, 29, 36, 37, 38, 39, 41, 55, 71, 73
federal funds, 56
federal government, 1, 4, 10, 11, 21, 23, 34, 35, 36, 37, 39, 41, 42, 45, 55, 56, 59
feedstock, 27
financial, 2, 3, 37, 39, 41, 59
financial stability, 59
fiscal policy, 36
fiscal year, 14, 36, 38, 39, 42, 50, 56, 74
food, 27
food safety, 27
Food, Conservation, and Energy Act of 2008, 37, 60
formula, 72
frost, 11
fruits, 6, 27, 39
funding, 20, 22, 27, 28
funds, 23, 24

G

GAO, 20, 33, 34, 40, 43, 44, 45, 47, 48, 52, 54, 62, 63, 64, 70, 71
Great Depression, 3, 72
growth, 14

H

health, 2
history, 9, 13, 29, 33, 37, 39, 40, 41, 42, 51, 60, 72
House, 28
hybrid, 7

I

identification, 58
identity, 14
income, vii, 1, 3, 14, 28, 29, 36, 40, 71, 74
income support, vii, 1, 3
industry, 2, 5, 7, 28, 34, 38, 50, 61
inflation, 23, 25
insects, 11
institutions, 28
insurance policy, 7, 27
integrity, 39
internal controls, 38, 63
investment, 50, 55
Iowa, 10
issues, 30

L

legislation, 28, 36, 38, 41
livestock, 2, 3, 6, 11, 29
loans, 3
low risk, 74

M

management, 38, 74
marketing, 72
median, 42
methodology, 8, 37, 38, 41, 51, 58, 60, 62, 73
mission, 38
modifications, 28
moisture, 3, 11, 16, 30, 36

N

NAP, 7, 30
natural disaster(s), 3, 41, 49, 55
neutral, 22

O

Office of the Inspector General, 38, 62, 73
officials, 34, 38, 46, 58, 60, 61, 62, 63
Oklahoma, 6
operating costs, 2, 4
operations, 14, 17, 71

P

pasture, 5, 19
percentile, 71, 74
policy, 1, 2, 4, 7, 9, 10, 11, 13, 14, 20, 21, 23, 27, 28, 29, 36, 41
policy makers, 2, 28
portfolio, 29, 30
poultry, 27
President, 36
price mechanism, 3
principles, 59
private sector, 3
producers, vii, 1, 3, 4, 6, 7, 11, 13, 21, 23, 27, 39
production costs, 27
profit, 24
protection, 10, 11, 23, 28, 29, 42, 49

R

rainfall, 6, 16
rangeland, 5
recommendations, 71
Reform, 29
regulations, 37, 60
reimburse, 3, 27
reinsurance, 21, 22, 23, 29, 31
reliability, 38, 63
relief, 42
renewable energy, 27
requirements, 23, 28
resources, 50, 55
response, 51, 73
revenue, vii, 1, 2, 4, 7, 8, 9, 10, 11, 13, 14, 15, 23, 27, 30, 36, 46, 61, 71, 72, 74
risk(s), vii, 1, 2, 3, 4, 6, 7, 21, 22, 23, 24, 25, 28, 30, 33, 34, 35, 36, 37, 38, 39, 42, 43, 44, 45, 46, 47, 48, 49, 50, 51, 52, 53, 54, 55, 56, 57, 58, 59, 60, 61, 62, 64, 71, 72, 73, 74
risk management, vii, 1, 4, 28
roots, 3
rules, 42

S

safety, vii, 1, 2, 3, 6, 28, 34, 35, 39, 55
savings, 4, 29, 50
SCO, 11, 27, 28, 31
scope, 29, 38
seed, 7
Senate, 28, 35, 36
shade, 44

shortfall, 11, 14
showing, 59, 72
signs, 4
simulation, 59
South Dakota, 6
soybeans, 2, 3, 4, 10, 11, 14, 16, 18, 19, 37, 39, 43, 44, 45, 47, 48, 51, 60, 61, 64, 73
specialty crop, 2, 6, 14, 27
species, 50
spending, 21, 42
stability, 38, 51, 56, 73
stakeholders, 34, 38, 61
state(s), 18, 23, 24, 25, 28, 38, 58, 59, 61, 71
statutes, 37, 60
structure, 15, 49
Subsidies, 10, 14, 15, 17, 19, 20, 47, 71
subsidy, 3, 14, 15, 17, 18, 19, 21, 26, 27, 29, 36, 41, 42, 46, 49, 55, 72
sugar beet, 19

T

target, 2, 13, 28, 31, 37, 39, 40, 41, 42, 43, 44, 45, 47, 48, 51, 52, 53, 54, 55, 56, 58, 59, 60, 61, 64, 71, 72, 73, 74
taxpayers, 2
time frame, 45, 46, 47
tobacco, 19
total costs, 17, 21, 59
transparency, 39

U

U.S. Department of Agriculture (USDA), vii, 1, 4, 5, 6, 9, 10, 21, 22, 24, 25, 30, 34, 35, 56, 60, 65, 73
underwriting, 21, 22, 25, 26, 29, 40, 45
United States, v, 16, 33, 35, 47
USDA, 1, 4, 6, 7, 9, 11, 16, 17, 18, 19, 22, 25, 27, 29, 30, 31, 33, 34, 35, 36, 37, 40, 41, 42, 43, 44, 45, 47, 48, 50, 51, 52, 54, 55, 57, 60, 61, 62, 63, 64, 72, 73

V

variations, 45, 58
vegetables, 6, 27, 39

W

Washington, 29, 30, 70, 71, 73
welfare, 38

Y

yield, vii, 1, 2, 4, 6, 7, 8, 9, 10, 11, 13, 15, 23, 39, 42, 46, 59, 61, 71, 72, 74